EXTRATERRESTRIAL SANDS

Laurence

All the best

George Gilligan

EXTRATERRESTRIAL SANDS

Part of the 'God King Scenario' Series

GARY GILLIGAN

WWW.GKS.UK.COM

Matador
9 Priory Business Park,
Wistow Road, Kibworth Beauchamp,
Leicestershire. LE8 0RX
Tel: 0116 279 2299
Email: books@troubador.co.uk
Web: www.troubador.co.uk/matador
Twitter: @matadorbooks

ISBN 978 1785891 694

British Library Cataloguing in Publication Data.
A catalogue record for this book is available from the British Library.

Printed and bound by CPI Group (UK) Ltd, Croydon, CR0 4YY
Typeset in 11pt Aldine401 BT by Troubador Publishing Ltd, Leicester, UK

Matador is an imprint of Troubador Publishing Ltd

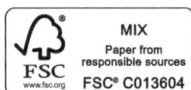

MIX
Paper from
responsible sources
FSC
www.fsc.org
FSC® C013604

Contents

INTRODUCTION

Catastrophism states that our Solar System has undergone a radical upheaval in the history of man and now exists as a smoking gun of recent cosmic chaos. It proposes that the Earth has been affected in the past by sudden, short-lived, violent events, which were worldwide in scope.

I have been a catastrophist author for a number of years now and under the umbrella title of the God King Scenario have published two books, *An Ancient World in Chaos* and *Comet Venus*. Both are available through my website, www.gks.uk.com, where many other related articles can be found.

To date, most of my work has been centred on the enigmatic Ancient Egyptians. The reason for this is very simple. I contend that every aspect of Egyptian life was dictated by catastrophic events in the heavens. Every tomb and temple façade, the length and breadth of the Nile Valley, records a time when the planets Mars, Venus, Mercury and the Moon danced with the Earth.

My previous writings provide a wealth of information on how catastrophism is not hidden away in some obscure cherry-picked interpretation or a figment of Egyptian imagination. On the contrary, it is in plain sight for all to see – the Egyptians have effectively laid the whole thing out for us. The very reason why this weird and wonderful world appears so alien to us is because catastrophism lies at the very heart of it.

My third book in the God King Scenario series presents a complete contrast to any previous research. I intend to demonstrate how the geological evidence is equally compelling and synchronises well with my Egyptian studies. *Extraterrestrial Sands* (ETS) is, as the title suggests, about sand raining down on Earth from the skies above.

The theory states that, historically, the planet Mars entered into hundreds of catastrophic close encounters with Earth. During these encounters an incandescent molten Mars internally convulsed and ejected immeasurable quantities of vaporised rock, volatiles, dust and debris out into space – a natural by-product of planetary chaos. Vast swathes of rock vapour fell to Earth (in addition to tons of other sedimentary material) where it condensed out of the atmosphere as minute quartz grains. In other words, it rained sand!

Earth has been subjected to a number of catastrophic sand and debris 'accretion events' in the past few thousand years and the evidence is obvious for all to see. It reaches us in the form of Earth's sandy deserts, beaches, dune fields and vast sandstone deposits. Quartz sand is anywhere and everywhere imaginable on the surface of the Earth, largely because it is extraterrestrial in origin. It is not the result of billions of years of erosion from basement rock as currently believed (uniformitarianism).

The geological task begins with an in-depth look at one of the largest and most well-known sandy deserts in the world, the Sahara. Here it will be shown how the origin of the sand is based on some seriously flawed assumptions – we don't actually know where the sand came from. Nobody, it seems, has had the foresight to look to the skies for answers… until now.

Sahara Desert

The Sahara is the world's largest hot desert and one of the harshest environments on the planet. It is the third largest desert, after Antarctica and the Arctic, which are cold deserts. At over 9,000,000 square kilometres (3,500,000 square miles), the Sahara covers most of North Africa, making it almost as large as the United States or the continent of Europe. The desert stretches from the Red Sea, including parts of the Mediterranean coasts, to the outskirts of the Atlantic Ocean.

Some of the sand dunes can reach 180 metres (600 feet) in height. Mixed in with the oceanic sands there are large rock formations, boulders, stones and pebbles. Contrary to popular belief, the desert is only 30 per cent sand. Some have compared areas of the Sahara to the surface of Mars. The sand alone from the great Saharan expanse could bury the entire world 8 inches deep (How the Earth Was Made: Season 2, Episode 4. Sahara) and is composed of almost pure quartz grains (silicon dioxide, $SiO2$). The reddish hue derives from a fine coating of iron oxide (which is rust coloured) on individual grains.

The Sahara's north-easterly winds can reach hurricane level and often give rise to sand storms and dust devils. Half of the Sahara receives less than an inch of rain per year, and the rest receives up to 4 inches (10 centimetres) per year. The infrequent rain is usually torrential.

The highest peak in the Sahara is the volcano Emi Koussi (11,204 feet or 3,415 metres) in the Tibesti Mountains in northern Chad. The desert's other mountains and mountain ranges include the Aïr Mountains, Hoggar (Ahaggar) Mountains, Saharan Atlas, Tibesti Mountains, Adrar des Iforas and the Red Sea hills.

The question is where does all the sand in the Sahara come from?

The light areas in the photo above show the wide swath of desert area that extends across Africa, the Middle East and the entire Asian continent. It encompasses many deserts including the Sahara & Arabian Deserts. For reasons that will become apparent later I have dubbed the vast swaths of sand deposited around the 30th parallel, "The Great Extraterrestrial Sand Scar."

The Great Extraterrestrial Sand Scar. Credit: NASA/Wikimedia.

Sahara – a sub-tropical paradise only 5,000 years ago

Although originally believed to have existed since time immemorial, recent discoveries reveal that the sands of the Sahara are hiding a big secret. It wasn't always a vast desolate forbidding place covered in sand – far from it. Around 5,000 years ago North Africa was teeming with life! It was a sub-tropical paradise where deer, hippos and elephants were hunted and giraffes, rhinoceros and lions roamed the area – a totally different world to that seen today – a place where large rivers, tributaries and lakes sustained a wide variety of fish and animals such as crocodiles. With a plentiful supply of food and water, thousands of hunter-gatherers flocked to settle in this lush green savannah. More recent research has shown that the once-green Sahara also hosted dairy farms. Saharan herders tended and milked livestock such as cattle, sheep and goats, processing the milk into products like yogurt, cheese and butter. (live science June 20, 2012)

The evidence for this hidden watery world comes to us via the discovery by ground-penetrating radar of hundreds of human graves and numerous rock paintings. Radar images taken by the NASA space shuttle show that beneath the sand lie a network of rivers and tributaries, which once spanned the whole Sahara.

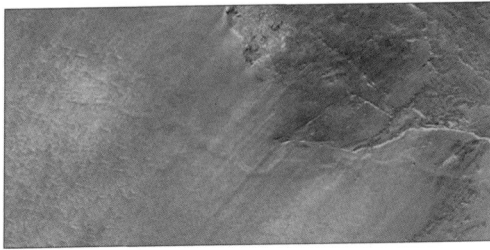
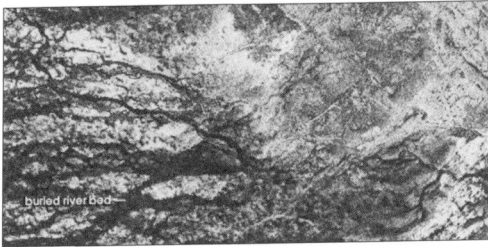

"Fossil rivers in the Sahara Desert, now buried by sand, attest to a much wetter climate in the past than now. Only a few faint stream channels are visible in the top image, a false-color scene from Landsat. Radar imagery (lower), which penetrates several meters beneath the sand, reveals a dense network of streambeds."

Source: http://earthobservatory.nasa.gov/Features/Paleoclimatology/

Petroglyphs and pictographs in the Jebel Acacus, Libyan Sahara.

Source: Carsten ten Brink

As can be seen in the above image, domesticated animals were clearly significant to Saharan people: the engraved and painted rock art found widely across the region includes many vivid representations of animals, particularly cattle. In some rare examples (not shown here), there are even scenes of milking and images of cows with full udders.

The Cave of Swimmers (circled), located in southwest Egypt, depicts a time when the Sahara was wetter.
Source: Roland Unger, Wikipedia.

What happened and when?

It is clearly evident that in the not-too-distant past large parts of the Sahara looked more like the Serengeti plains in East Africa – tree-pocked grasslands which supported a diversity of animals as well as a large human population. The question is – what happened to this lush green world? When and how did this once wet region turn to the most arid region on Earth?

It was initially believed the Sahara died out abruptly, about 5,000 years ago. However, a study published by Reuters in May 2008 suggested this is incorrect and that the process took millennia:

"The once-green Sahara turned to desert over thousands of years rather than in an abrupt shift as previously believed, according to a study on Thursday that may help understanding of future climate changes. The study of ancient pollen, spores and aquatic organisms in sediments in Lake Yoa in northern Chad showed the region gradually shifted from savannah 6,000 years ago towards the arid conditions that took over about 2,700 years ago. The findings, about one of the biggest environmental shifts of the past 10,000 years, challenge past belief based on evidence in marine sediments that a far quicker change created the world's biggest hot desert."

(Sahara dried out slowly, not abruptly: study.)

Precisely how – and how quickly – the region dried up has been a matter of scientific dispute and a more recent study is set to revolutionise our view of how the Sahara became a desert. In the magazine Science (October 2013), marine geologists Jessica Tierney and Peter deMenocal analysed ocean sediments of the Horn of Africa. What the scientists found was that, far from shifting gradually from wet to dry, the climate in the Horn of Africa changed in perhaps as little as 100 to 200 years, incredibly quickly in geological terms. (When the Sahara turned to sand less than 200 years. http://phys.org/news/2013-11-sahara-sand.html). This leads to another question – what sort of climate change could be responsible for such rapid desertification?

Earth's orbital change –
Milankovitch cycles

Milankovitch cycles refer to long-term changes in Earth's orbital and axial variations, which are thought to correlate with the Earth's climate over the course of hundreds of thousands, and even millions, of years of Earth's history. The cycles are considered to initiate long-term natural cycles of ice ages and warm eras known as glacial and interglacial periods.

Geologists and Egyptologists often cite the Milankovitch cycle (or more simply, a change in Earth's orbit) for the drying out of North Africa; it bodes well with the original relatively slow drying out proposal. However, the latest research really throws a spanner in the works.

> "The reason North Africa warmed up, they believe, was a cyclic change in Earth's orientation toward the sun (called precession) which caused more sunlight to fall during the Northern Hemisphere's summer. But the precession cycle is slow, taking 23,000 years to complete. So why was the changeover in the Horn of Africa so quick? (ibid)

> Previous research has suggested that the end of the African Humid Period came gradually, over thousands of years, but a study published last month in Science says it took just a few hundred. The shift was initially triggered by more sunlight falling on Earth's northern hemisphere, as Earth's cyclic

orientation toward the sun changed. But how that orbital change caused North Africa to dry out so fast – in 100 to 200 years, says the study – is a matter of debate." (phys.org 11, Nov 2013)

The Milankovitch cycle has to be dismissed as the probable cause for the drying out of the Sahara on the grounds that it favours a slow progression. The latest evidence doesn't support this – it shows the Sahara underwent a catastrophic transformation in less than the blink of an eye in geological terms. The Milankovitch model is repeatedly presented as fact – it is often called upon to explain past climatic change (such as the advance and retreat of the polar ice caps), yet when you scratch the surface it seems the hypothesis is really rather fragile. That said, regardless of whether the Sahara dried up gradually or suddenly, neither theory explains the appearance of so much sand – where did all the sand in the Sahara come from?

Drying out

It is perplexing how so much emphasis is placed on the "drying out" of the Sahara with little or no consideration as to the implications. For example, how does the "drying out" of vast regions produce such copious amounts of sand? The Sahara was once teeming with life and home to a large human population, which can only mean the soil was rich and fertile – how does this dry out to become sand? The verdant green Serengeti has been compared to the Sahara's last wet period – if we theoretically "dried out" its rich fertile soil, would it too turn to sand and create dunes 180 metres high? Of course not – soil does not dry out to become sand, a simple back-garden experiment can confirm this. In some areas of the Sahara the sand is so fine it is almost silk-like to the touch, and is thus thought to be among some of the oldest and finest sand in world, which has taken several million years to form. If correct, this raises the question as to how such vast, millennia-old oceans of pure pristine sand appeared this side of a 200-year "drying out" blip.

"Dried up" is an inadequate description for what was a huge catastrophic event that transformed a region comparable in size to the United States. Taking into account the latest research, hundreds of thousands of people either starved to death or were displaced (to the Nile Valley) in less than 200 years. Flora and fauna disappeared; some species have never been seen again. If the same fate were bestowed on the USA, would we be using the term "dried up"?

Sahara sand dunes. It's difficult to conceive how hidden beneath these vast sandy oceans lies a sub-tropical paradise. How does "drying out" produce such copious amounts of sand?

Source: fr: Utilisateur: Jgremillot, Wikimedia Commons.

Always there?

By way of an answer, Earth scientists suggest that the Sahara must have undergone several wet and dry periods over many millennia and that the sand accumulated to be largely present even through the more recent wet period. In other words, the desert has come and gone on a number of occasions. Scientists reason that sand takes many millions of years to form and, as such, it would be impossible for vast quantities to appear in the blink of an eye, so the sand must have been present throughout in some form or another. If this is correct, then it follows that what we see today (huge oceans of dunes in places) *must* be very close to what existed during the recent wet period, otherwise this would mean masses of sand somehow magically appeared.

A pre-existing sandy environment presents a number of problems, such as how a vibrant ecosystem could flourish if the land was dominated by vast quantities of sand. How did masses of people and animals, including cattle, cope in such a sandy environment? It was obviously very wet during this time, which means rain – and given the evidence, lots of it – so perhaps rain washed the sand away? Consulting the NASA radar images suggests this is highly unlikely if not impossible, for the images clearly reveal a vast network of lakes, rivers and tributaries infilled with layers of sand. How is this possible, if this was a lush, green, free-flowing watery world just a few thousand years ago? The timescale according to conventional thinking simply doesn't allow for such a rapid deposition of so much sand.

Early civilisations were based around rivers. Some common examples are Ancient Egypt (Nile), the Fertile Crescent (Tigris/Euphrates), Ancient China (Yellow River) and Ancient India (Indus). Water makes the land fertile for growing crops – goods and people can be transported, and people can hunt the animals that come to drink the water. They can catch fish in the rivers. Moreover, rivers provide a steady supply of drinking water and without these rivers ancient cultures would have perished (this is a fact). Prehistoric Saharan people no doubt followed suit and resided near water, but if the sand existed anywhere near the quantities seen today, fluvial processes would have washed the sand (silt/mud) into the streams and rivers (low-lying depressions) causing them to silt up. In other words, water, the very lifeblood of these early humans would have been cut off – it would have been the first to go, and without water they would not have been able to survive. The whole ecosystem would have failed. With this in mind, it begs the question as to how early farmers ever managed to get started in the first place if large quantities of sand existed during such times.

We will revisit the "sand existing for millennia" problem again shortly. Meanwhile, we turn out attention to the very important question of the actual provenance of the sand, that is to say the primary origin of the quartz grains. Although very much a grey area it is my intention to clarify the situation and dispel many erroneous assumptions. As will become apparent, the provenance of the sand remains *unknown*!

Desert sands – in search of provenance

Although the encyclopedia.org/Sahara webpage no longer exists, the following is often quoted by those who are not prepared to probe a little further on the question of provenance. (Please note: sandstone is sand that has been lithified, i.e. turned to rock. Most sand grains of most sandstones are quartz. Granite is a common type of felsic intrusive igneous rock [crystallised from molten magma].)

"The sand is primarily derived from weathering of Cretaceous sandstones in North Africa. When these sandstones were deposited in the Cretaceous, the area where they are now was a shallow sea. The original source of the sand was the large mountain ranges that still exist in the central part of the Sahara. These mountains are volcanic and intrusive, and the granite rock weathers out to leave behind quartz sand grains that are carried by rivers to the sea. These sand deposits eventually formed into sandstone, and as they were uplifted began to weather and break down into sand again."
https://uk.answers.yahoo.com/question/index?qid=20060728160828AA8pP6m

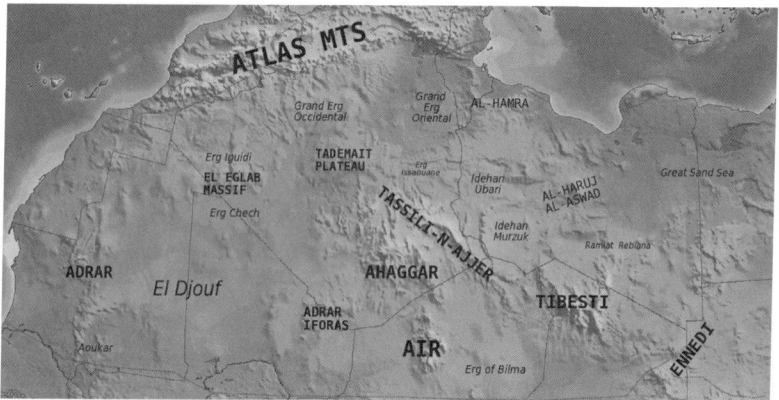

Map showing major dune seas (ergs) and mountain ranges of the Sahara. The Atlas Mountains are to the north while the central mountains consist of the Tebesti and Ahaggar (Hogger) massifs.

Source: T L Miles Wikimedia.

I wrote to Professor of Sedimentology Charles Bristow at Birkbeck University of London and questioned the above premise: "Are the mountain ranges in the central part of the Sahara the source of the sand?" He disputes this and provides an explanation as to why:

"The modern mountains are of little consequence. The Atlas is largely an inverted rift basin much of which is Tethyan realm carbonates and other sedimentary rocks. The Tibesti mountains are basaltic volcanoes which are geologically very young. Their erosion would not produce quartz sand anyway. [...] The Hoggar and other cratonic areas are more likely to be sediment sources."

It is evident the mountains in the Sahara are *not* the source of the sand. Bristow further suggests the origin probably lies with sandstone deposits in the south: "The source of the Sahara sand is most likely to be the underlying Nubian sandstones."

As well as notifying us of the unknown provenance, the following most up-to-date excerpt also suggests a probable Nubian Sandstone origin:

"In many instances, the source of the sand is not clear or not known. The high degree of mineralogical maturity of sand from Libyan sand seas (Muhs, 2004) suggests long-distance transport, repeated periods of transport and reworking over short distances, or a source in the mineralogically mature Nubian

Sandstone that crops out extensively in the eastern Sahara."
Encyclopedia of Quaternary Science, 2nd Edition, Elias & Mock, 2013

Given the colossal amounts of sand involved, it is bewildering that we cannot determine its origin. Is it possible that consensus thinking has blinded scientists to something much more obvious?

Sahara dunes at sunset. Pristine deposits of sand?
Source: Wikimedia Commons.

Farouk El-Baz – a provenance thesis

We turn our attention to eminent geologist Farouk El-Baz, who, as far as I am aware, was probably the first to propose the Nubian Sandstone origin. El-Baz, apart from participating in the Apollo Program for NASA, has spent many years studying arid environments, particularly the Great Sahara of North Africa and the Arabian Peninsula, in addition to other features of the Earth and its oceans. He is credited with providing evidence that the desert is the result of major climatic variations. Based on the interpretation of the NASA radar images (above), it was El-Baz who uncovered the numerous sand-buried rivers and streams in the Sahara. He has written many papers on the subject and appeared in a number of documentaries. (For more information on El-Baz http://www.bu.edu/remotesensing/faculty/el-baz/.)

El-Baz has formulated his theory over some twenty years plus, a summary of which is below.

> "The Great Sahara of North Africa encompasses the largest number of sand dune fields in any desert. Massive dunes in numerous patterns cover large areas of the terrain. Many of the dune fields of the Great Sahara occur within or near topographic depressions. This fact must be explained in any theory regarding the origin of the sand and the evolution of dune forms in space and time. **It is here proposed that the dune sand originated by fluvial erosion of sandstone rocks such as those of the Nubian Sandstone to the south of, or close to the present sand seas.** The rounding of grains must

have occurred in turbid water as the particulate matter was transported during humid phases in the courses of now dry rivers and streams. The sediment load must have been deposited in low areas at the mouths of these channels. During dry climates, the particulate matter was exposed to the action of wind, which sculptured the sand into various dune forms depending on the amount of available sand and prevailing wind directions." [Author's bold emphasis]

http://www.bu.edu/remotesensing/files/pdf/398.pdf

In proposing the Nubian Sandstone origin El-Baz also dismisses any rocks to the north: "The exposed rocks to the north of the sand seas are mostly limestones, of Eocene or younger ages, which could not have been the source of the vast amounts of sand." (ibid. p. 14)

Nubian Sandstone outcrop formation, the Amram Columns, Eilat Massif, Israel.

Source: User: Doron, Wikimedia Commons

Nubian Sandstone refers to a variety of sedimentary rocks deposited on the Precambrian Basement in the Eastern Sahara, north-east Africa and Arabia. It consists of continental sandstones with thin beds of marine limestone, and marls. Nubian Sandstone was deposited between the Lower Paleozoic and Upper Cretaceous, with marine beds dating from the Carboniferous to Lower Cretaceous (Nubian Sandstone, Wiki). Nubian sandstone underlies an extensive area of Egypt. Throughout the southern part of the Eastern Sahara it is largely exposed; to the north it is mainly overlain with carbonate rocks and a covering of sand.

Recent exploration has revealed huge reservoirs of water located underground in the eastern end of the Sahara Desert. Known as The Nubian Sandstone Aquifer System (NSAS), it is the world's largest known fossil water aquifer system. NSAS covers a land area spanning just over two million square kilometres, including north-western Sudan, north-eastern Chad, south-eastern Libya and most of Egypt. Containing an estimated 150,000 cubic kilometres of groundwater, the significance of the NSAS as a potential water resource for future development programmes in these countries is extraordinary. It is believed many of the aquifers underneath were last filled with water during the Sahara's last wet period. Due to the lack of rainwater in the region this is a non-renewable water resource. In simplistic terms when it's gone, it's gone.

In short, El-Baz (as others) is proposing that the Sahara has undergone several wet and dry episodes over many millennia. Wet periods saw fluvial processes (lots of rain) erode away exposed sandstone rocks in the south, which migrated north via rivers and tributaries towards the Mediterranean following the general lay of the land. The sand accumulated at the mouths of these channels and lakebeds. Alternating dry climatic episodes resulted in sculpturing the deposits into dunes and sheets by the southward-flowing wind – a process that continues today.

El-Baz's peers seem to be open to the basic premise of a Nubian Sandstone origin. However, in 1998 Prof. Dr. Rushdi Said published a paper entitled "Sand accumulation and ground water in the eastern Sahara: A rebuttal to El-Baz". Said accuses El-Baz of ignoring the early pioneering works of Ralf Bagnold (1896–1990) and others who believe that the dune fields were formed during the last ice age when North Africa was arid and the sea level was lower. That is to say, they favoured a more 'localised' northern sand source. Rather than present the whole paper I think it would be a good idea to take a look at the relevant excerpt from El-Baz's reply. It is self-explanatory and offers further evidence that 'the rocks in the north could not have been the source'. To my knowledge there was no counter-riposte.

"There is no objection to the formation of sand dunes during the last glacial. Sand in the form of dunes and sand-sheets however, continues to accumulate at present. To invoke the origin of the sand from "the fetches of the exposed continental shelf which extended into the Mediterranean Sea at places for more than forty kilometers" requires unreasonable assumptions, because: (1) most of the shelf facies of the southern Mediterranean basin arc composed of carbonates and lowering the sea level by 120m would only expose more carbonates; sand in the Western Desert is over 90 percent quartz (El-Baz, et al. 1979, p. 254), which cannot be derived from the coastal Mediterranean: and (2) deriving sand from the continental shelf and transporting it uphill for hundreds of meters and then upslope for hundreds of kilometers to its present location would require a wind regime with untenable velocities. The fluvial origin of the sand from vast exposures of Nubian Sandstone in the southern pan of the desert requires the least number of assumptions."

http://www.bu.edu/remotesensing/files/pdf/492.pdf

Has El-Baz discovered the source? Was the sand born by water and later shaped by the wind? By taking a closer look it will be shown that there are a number of fundamental problems with El-Baz's thesis.

The image below shows the location of the main dune fields in the North African Sahara. The arrows fanning out from the north-east towards the south–south east represent the general direction of the dunes as dictated by the prevailing winds. The bold 'oval' shape denotes El-Baz's proposed location for the Saharan sand which is in the south-west part of the Western Desert of "Egypt" (not to be confused with the Western Desert of the "Sahara" which designates the west part of North Africa). The large bold arrows pointing north represent the proposed northern flow of the original water-eroded sands. And of course, not shown, but hidden beneath the sand, we have the network of ancient rivers and tributaries.

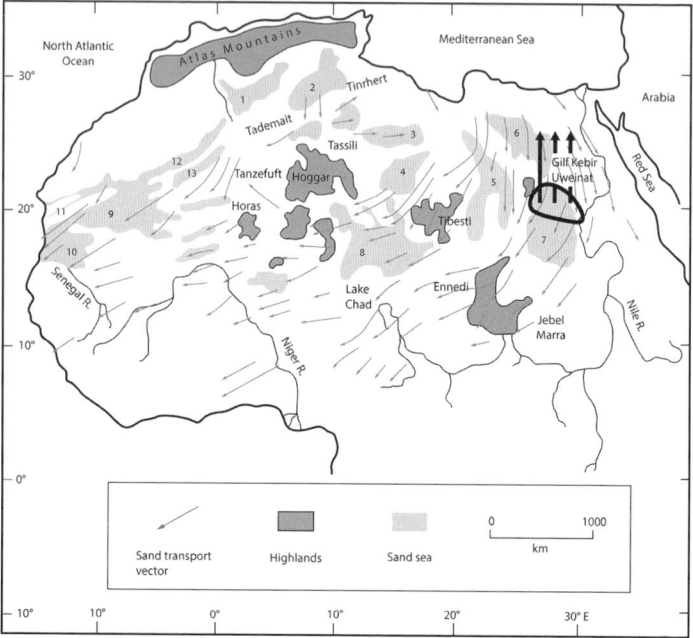

Sahara sand seas and vectors of sand transport. The 'oval' shape and the three large arrows represent Farouk El-Baz's proposed underlying source and direction of sand during times past. The sand seas are numbered as follows: 1. Grand Erg Occidental, 2. Grand Erg Oriental, 3. Ubari, 4. Muzuq, 5. Calanscio, 6. Great Sand Sea, 7. Selima Sand Sheet, 8. Fachi-Bilma & Tenere, 9. Majabat al Koubra, 10. Akchar, 12. Iguidi and 13, Chech.

Source: Author.

Working back and looking at the broader picture here, El-Baz is basically saying that the majority of sand we see today began life as sandstone in the south-west corner of Egypt's western desert. To put this into some kind of perspective, it is estimated that the dunes today cover an area of nearly 2.5 million square kilometres – a vast, vast area. The United Kingdom would fit into this just over ten times. The area (not volume) covered by the Himalayan Mountains would fit into the dune area over two times – compare this to El-Baz's proposed location for the sands origin (the Nubian Sandstone outcrops as in the image above). This covers an area of approximately 233,000 square kilometres and is about one tenth (10.71 per cent) of the total sand area. Taking the sand area as a whole would require shrinking it by about 90 per cent to make it fit. This is one helluva lot of sand to compress back into the relatively small region of Egypt's south-western corner. If we were to reinstate the sand, what sort of height would we be looking at?

As we know, if we were to take all the sand in the Sahara it would bury the Earth to a depth of 20 centimetres (8 inches) and since Earth's surface area is 510 million square kilometres this gives us 102,000 cubic kilometres of sand (area multiplied by depth). If we now divide the volume by the area of 233,000 square kilometres it equates to a height of roughly 438 metres. Considering that the Empire State building stands at 381 metres, this would mean an imposing sandstone complex of colossal proportions must have once existed here. And let's be clear, such a complex could only have stood at some considerable elevation, otherwise perpetual erosion by rainwater could not have taken place.

Did a colossal sandstone "mountain" once tower over this region? El-Baz provides little in the way of evidence or information here; we are certainly not afforded any images and to date nothing has been done in the way of provenance, which is very puzzling. We turn to Google Earth (and the locational photos pinned within), which reveals the region to be very flat with numerous rocky outcrops (some very large) protruding into a landscape dominated by sand, rocks and pebbles. The area shows signs of severe denudation but this is true of all parts of the Sahara – one rocky outcrop looks pretty much like another. Although it's impossible to perceive, the land slopes down towards the south following the general north–south lay of the land.

It is without doubt, the region appears vast; indeed any people shown in the Google photos appear dwarfed by the hostile landscape. However, this doesn't compare to the enormous areas covered by the sand as a whole. At 2.5 million square kilometres by area and 102,000 cubic kilometres by volume we are dealing with almost unimaginable quantities. With this in mind, shouldn't the evidence be unequivocal if this is indeed the place of origin? After all, the region was extremely wet (saturated) for many millennia right up until 5,000 years ago. If a colossal sandstone deposit existed here it must have undergone ceaseless erosion by rainwater, right up until very recently. We would therefore expect to see solid physical evidence of masses of sand emanating from this location – a clear directional and quantitative source pattern with clear definitive and defining features. We don't see this; in fact it doesn't look that much different to many other areas of the Sahara. Is 5,000 years really enough to disguise such a vast sand source? Sounds highly unlikely.

As mentioned earlier, Nubian Sandstone underlies an extensive area of Egypt. In addition to the outcrops some believe such deposits may have also participated in the production of Saharan sand. This is puzzling, for how could rain possibly erode away "underlying" sandstone? Any underlying sandstone would have been naturally shielded from erosion by overlying sand, exactly as it is today. Perhaps the "underlying" was "overlying" (or at least large regions exposed) at some point in the past, but if this was the case, when? Were plate tectonics a factor here? Was the land originally higher or perhaps thrust up only to settle back down again to its current level? Due to the lack of microscopic seashells (freshwater shells do exist) mixed in with the sand grains, it is now known that the Sahara could not have been a sea bed as some Victorians believed – so where does that leave us? Does any of this relate with the proposed timescale for when the sandstone was initially laid down? It's all very vague and confusing but if scientists are going to pin their allegiance to such an idea, then at the very least what we could expect is some kind of plausible working model. After all, we're dealing with mind-boggling quantities of sand – how can we not know where it came from?

North-east corner?

Moving on through the cycle, El-Baz suggests that during the wet episodes colossal amounts of sand were washed north from Egypt's south-west corner via rivers, and this sand settled around the mouths of rivers and lakebeds. During the alternating dry episodes the prevailing wind took over and transported the sand back in a south–southwesterly direction to somehow fan out across the whole of the Sahara.

It is difficult to ascertain how any of this would work, especially when taking into account the quantities of sand, the timescale and the fact that none of the paleo-rivers flow out into the sea. Any wet episodes would see the rivers and lakes rapidly silt up, perhaps within a few decades. This would, of course, depend on erosion rates but to get to the volumes of sand observed today, this must have been absolutely unremitting. A contributing factor in siltation would be the tons of mud and organic material washed off the once fertile land. This would mix with the sand to silt up the lakes followed by the streams feeding them, but how does this correlate with the verdant world that once existed here? Water, the very source of life, would be cut off in the very first instance.

By way of an analogy we turn to Ramesses II's great capital, Pi-Ramesses, built around 1,300 BC (conventional chronology). Boasting a population of 300,000 and covering some 30 square kilometres Pi-Ramesses was dominated by palatial estates, a massive temple complex, and the royal palace. It was situated along an extensive system of canals and lakes in the eastern Nile Delta (about 60 miles north-east of Cairo) and would have been one of the glories of the ancient world. Pi-Ramesses remained in full bloom for over a century until it simply vanished. What happened? The branch of the Nile on which Pi-Ramesses was built, the Pelusiac, silted up causing the river to change course. Egypt's once crowning jewel was left with no source of water

– consequently, Pi-Ramesses was abandoned. It is believed the Nile has changed course a number of times in the past.

It's only a small point but a point worth mentioning. A once thriving city died because a branch of the Nile silted up and changed course – the mighty Egyptians were brought to their knees by a lack of water. Wouldn't the ancient rivers and lakes have succumbed to similar siltation processes? It is logical to assume even more so because unlike the Nile, which flushes out into the Mediterranean, the ancient streams are interior streams, i.e. they flow into inland basins; they do not flow to the sea and are thus more prone to siltation.

After being deposited in the north-east by water the dry episodes saw the sand grains migrate south–south-west via the wind. It further accumulates in low-lying depressions (rivers etc.) blanketing the land, not too dissimilar to what is seen today. There doesn't seem to be much wrong with this supposition. However, the problems arise with the onset of a wet episode in that gravity would take its course transporting the sand back north. This has to be so otherwise the land could not have supported the once thriving world hidden beneath the sands.

Due to the extreme wet conditions and as water is a more powerful transporter of sand than wind (rivers consist of moving water going downhill which has more kinetic energy and momentum than wind), the watery journey north would be quicker than the wind-driven journey *uphill* south. Once more, this has to be so for it cannot have been both ways – either the region was extremely wet with heaps of rainwater eroding away at the source transporting it south or dryer conditions prevailed. And if it was dry, we then lose the water-borne source of the sand. With this in mind it begs the question as to how such enormous quantities of sand managed to escape the north-east corner to spread out south across the whole of North Africa. Considering the lack of flow to the ocean, once more the sand, silt and mud would just slowly accumulate in Africa's north-east corner.

The North Wind doth blow!

The image above (page No.22) shows the direction of the sand as dictated by the prevailing wind which has blown from the north-east for at least half a million years, or so we're led to believe. You will also note two large dune areas situated near the Atlas Mountains to the north-west. These are known as the Grand Erg Occidental (or Great Western Erg) and the Grand Erg Oriental (Great Eastern Erg), respectively (Sand ergs 1 & 3 in the image above). They consist of vast oceans of sand rising hundreds of metres high and cover great swathes of landscape, mainly in Algeria. The Occidental measures some 80,000 square kilometres, the Oriental is much larger at 120,000.

There is an obvious problem here that needs to be addressed, and that is how such vast deposits of sand managed to accumulate so far north when the prevailing wind blows from the north-east. It makes little sense. In fact, if we adopt El-Baz's premise that the sand flowed from the north-east region of the Sahara it becomes an impossible situation – the north wind just wouldn't allow for the build-up of so much sand in this region. A point affirmed when considering both ergs are situated at higher latitudes than the Great Sand Sea (72,000 square kilometres) in the north-east, the supposed source of the wind-borne sand.

No matter how you look at it, the transportation of so much sand to the Sahara's northern regions by the wind just doesn't add up – such deposits shouldn't exist if the wind has blown from the north for half a million years or so – but if the wind wasn't responsible, then what was? Perhaps it arrived there via the old network of streams and tributaries? There is absolutely no evidence for this whatsoever. If there were, it would have shown up on the radar images. It is difficult to conceive of any theory that would explain the origin of the Occidental and Oriental ergs. As with the whole of the Sahara, it looks as though the sand was literally dumped on top of North Africa.

A Circular Problem – a glimpse into the future?

It matters little as to how many "millions of years" scientists attempt to ascribe to the cycles of the Sahara or where they place them in time and space, it is very apparent we have a recurring circular problem, since the more it rains the more erosion takes place and the more erosion, the more the rivers and lakes silt up (and the more the source areas become shielded). A consequence of this would be a sand-dominated environment unconducive to life – how is that possible?

Let us look at this another way: unless scientists are suggesting that the alternating wet and dry cycles have now ceased, then we are currently amidst a dry period. Now, what would happen if we were to theoretically wind the clock forward to the next wet episode – a time when, as before, North Africa is once again subjected to a plentiful supply of rainwater? Would the region transform itself back to how it was only a few thousand years ago – a world teeming with life and where people hosted dairy farms? Given enough time and plenty of water, areas of little sand would no doubt turn green again, probably quite rapidly, but what of the sand? Where would all the sand go?

It stands to reason that gravity would see the sand ultimately wash into low-lying areas, which as we know would be the same location as the ancient rivers and lakes now hidden beneath the sand. Once again, since no outflow to the sea exists, the sand would just build up and up, further accumulating in areas already filled with sand. Would the paleo-rivers ever free-flow again, as before? Given the enormous quantities of sand involved I would suggest this to be near impossible. Perhaps new river paths would be cut providing an outlet to the sea or maybe an "overflow" system would develop, flushing out into the River Nile. Either way, it just wouldn't be the same as before.

As stated earlier, the leading model deems the sand to have existed for several thousand, if not millions of years – it has remained through many wet and dry episodes and what we see today isn't that much different to what existed 10,000 years ago, or so it is believed. The above brief step into the future highlights the serious recurring flaw in this premise. In that, the clogging up of the rivers and lakes *must* have also occurred with the onset of the last wet episode – a logical assumption if the sand has "always been there". What this means is the world beneath the sands could not have existed in the same form as presented by the recent evidence – a verdant green world with streams unclogged by sand. How can this be possible?

Some may suggest that over millennia the ancient lakes and rivers would gradually clear, giving rise to a free-flowing watery world; this has to be a nonstarter, unless it can be shown, not only how the erosional process ceased during wet episodes and how large amounts of sand dispersed from low-lying areas, but also how it magically and suddenly reappeared with the onset of the current dry episode. Considering again that the most basic of formulas – the more it rains = more erosion = more sand accumulation in rivers and lakes – it is clear, no matter how you look at it, that it makes no sense.

Selima Sand Sheet

Great quantities of sand not only cover the whole of the proposed source area but also blanket the land in all directions, especially to the south. This can be seen by taking a look at the Selima Sand Sheet (sand sea No 7 in the image above), which occupies 60,000 square kilometres in southern Egypt and northern Sudan. As one of the Earth's largest sand sheets the Selima is absolutely flat in a few places. In others, active dunes move over its surface. The northern part of the Selima covers more than half of the proposed source area – it spans out well to the south covering an area of roughly 30,000 square kilometres. Sandy desert conditions also prevail well to the south beyond the Selima for several kilometers (https://en.wikipedia.org/wiki/Aeolian_processes).

How did such large quantities of sand accumulate so far south of the proposed source? Did fluvial processes play a part here? On this, El-Baz and others are understandably silent as there doesn't seem to be any evidence for this. If there were, it would contradict said thesis. Perhaps the sand flowed north during the wet episodes only to be blown back south beyond the source area during the dry spells? The main problem with this is the timescale – the Selima Sand Sheet, according to the consensus view, is between 20,000 and 15,000 years old (Dunes: Dynamics, Morphology, History. 2013 Warren p 90). This takes it right back through and beyond the last wet episode – how is that possible if this is the source area? Was the area drenched in water or not? If it was, then the sand sheet cannot be 20,000, 10,000 or even 15,000 years old. Indeed, logic dictates it can only be 3,000 or 4,000 years old – laid down during and after the last wet episode. But hold on – if erosion and deposition takes many tens of thousands of years, how did the sand appear in such a short space of time? And round and round we go!

Maybe post-aeolian processes eroded away the sandstone outcrops and blew them south?

There is no doubt aeolian processes have played and continue to play a part in shaping the Sahara, this is not called into question. However, once again the time frame just doesn't allow for a post wind-based process. It would take many tens of thousands of years (and more) for the wind to erode away the quantities of sand seen today in and around the source area. This would further contradict that Selima has existed for 20,000 years.

Aeolian or fluvial deposition?

In regards to the location of dunes with respect to depressions the following was taken from a paper titled "Evolution of Sand Seas", written by El-Baz in 1992.

"Mainguet (1984) also observed that most ergs occur near depressions. However, they do not occur in the lowest part, but on a slightly higher slope. Based on prevailing theories, she ascribed the formation of erg dunes to aeolian deposition. However, it is here proposed that the accumulation of the sand began in depressions that received water and suspended sediments during pluvial. The shape of these accumulations changed when the desert environment dried up and aeolian action became a significant agent of particle transport. As the sand grains were moved by the winds, dune formation commenced, sometimes on slightly high slopes. As this process continued, the lowest parts of the depressions were, in some cases, left sand-free."

The above clearly reveals the dunes aren't where they're supposed to be... where the water left them, in the lowest part of the depressions. This has led to El-Baz to suggest *"aeolian action"* moved the sand grains onto slopes with the onset of the last dry episode (or at least during dry episodes). Given the timescale and the enormous quantities of sand involved this has to downright impossible. Let us remember the Sahara was transformed rapidly into a barren desert only 5,000 years ago and according to consensus view what we see today hasn't altered much since this time. Yet here we are expected to believe tons upon tons of quartz sand jumped out of depressions onto higher slopes during this catastrophic transitional period of less than 200 years.

Drawing the reader's attention to *any* image where some of the large sand dunes are shown, it's not too difficult to determine just how implausible this sounds. Furthermore, if this was indeed what occurred wouldn't the evidence be a bit more obvious, enough perhaps to cause Mainguet to be more sympathetic towards El-Baz's thesis? This is clearly not the case. In addition to this, if *"the accumulation of the sand began in depressions that received water,"* then, as pointed out many times now, the lost verdant world beneath could not have flourished. This really is the crux of the matter when dealing with the origin of the sand; any proposal has to correspond with the latest evidence which shows the Sahara underwent a catastrophic and rapid transformation in as little as a hundred years. I would suggest here Mainguet is on the right path, the sand was the result of aeolian deposition, but not in a way she could have ever imagined.

Summary

It is plain to see there is something clearly amiss when it comes to providing answers as to where all the sand in the Sahara came from. Most people are all too hasty to cite the apparent orthodox view that on closer inspection just doesn't add up or in most cases is just plain wrong. A prime example would be the erroneous assumption (still blindly perpetuated) that the sand originated from central mountains in the Sahara.

The discovery of the watery world beneath the sand has prompted El-Baz to formulate his own model and it's not that difficult to see how this originated. Armed with the customary "billions of years" frame of mind (how can they possibly know!), El-Baz has concluded, like so many, that sand must be indigenous to the African continent. This has led him to the largest (not least of) mainly exposed sandstone deposits in the Eastern Sahara – it follows since sand originates from sandstone, this is where the sand must have originated – a seemingly natural conclusion within the confines of orthodoxy. But far from discovering the source, El-Baz has only succeeded in highlighting the problems of origin. The notion that the sand originated from Egypt's south-west corner is tenuous at best. It is based on many assumptions rather than physical evidence since there are no definitive features, no geographical characteristics that stand out and lead us to believe that the sand initially flowed from "El-Baz's corner" Added to this the fact that most dunes do not occur at the lowest parts of the depressions it's difficult to ascribe merit to El-Baz's thesis. But if we dismiss Farouk's thesis where does this leave us? Let me put this as succinctly as possible: the Sahara Desert's sand provenance... UNKNOWN!

Given the quantities of sand involved this is a situation that absolutely should not exist; how can we not know? We have a geological "sand scar" that can be seen from space but has no confirmed origin. To all intents and purposes it looks as though vast swathes of sand have been literally dumped on top of North Africa (and the Arabian Peninsular, which we will discuss next), and quite recently. Could this indeed be the case? Is it possible that scholars have got this one completely wrong and what we are looking at here is an extraterrestrial deposit – vast clouds of quartz grains that rained down and literally smothered a region that was once a sub-tropical paradise? I believe so, but before we delve into a thesis that will test even the most open-minded person, let us take a look at another vast sandy desert, Sahara's neighbouring desert of Arabia. As I will demonstrate, we have yet more vast sandy oceans of unknown origin.

THE ARABIAN DESERT – ANOTHER SUB-TROPICAL PARADISE ONLY 5,000 YEARS AGO?

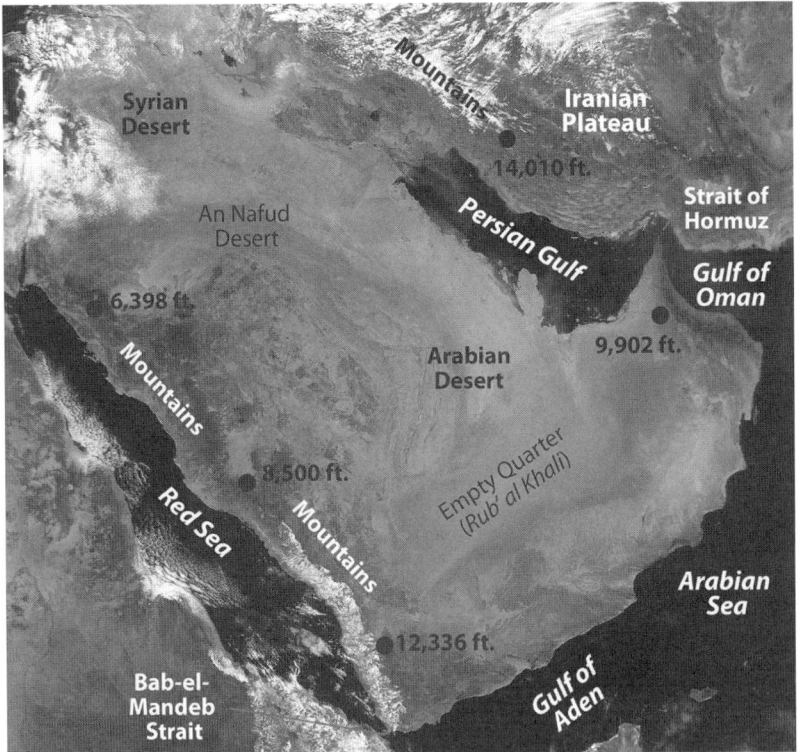

Arabian Desert: Witch forms part of the ET sand scar. Note the Empty Quarter (Rub al Khali) in the south.

Source: Wikimedia Commons.

The Arabian Desert is located in Western Asia. It is a vast desert wilderness stretching from Yemen to the Persian Gulf and Oman to Jordan and Iraq. It occupies most of the Arabian Peninsula. Sand seas or ergs are one of the most prominent physiographic features and cover about 770,000 square kilometres or almost one-third of the Arabian Peninsula's land surface. Nearly 90 percent of this sand is contained in three sand seas: the An Nafud (also called the Great Nafud), located in north-central Saudi Arabia; the Rub al Khali, located in southern and south-eastern Arabia; and the Ad Dahna, a 1,200-km-long, curvilinear belt of dunes that connects the first two sand seas. Together these sand seas form the largest continuous body of quartz sand in the world. The variety of dune shapes and sizes are vast and many forms have not even been described in print. As with the Sahara similar inhospitable hyperarid conditions prevail.

Arabia wasn't always a vast desolate forbidding place covered in sand – far from it! In fact, direct comparisons can be made with the Sahara desert in that NASA images have revealed a similar network of ancient river valleys and lake basins under the sands.

> "Satellite images have revealed that a network of ancient rivers once coursed their way through the sand of the Arabian Desert, leading scientists to believe that the region experienced wetter periods in the past."
> (Phys.org May 2012)

Water, of course, means life and the following confirms Arabia was once a verdant paradise that supported a diverse community of animals, similar to the Sahara.

> "Fossil evidence shows that in the late Miocene there were lush riverine valleys in the west of Abu Dhabi with savannahs populated by elephant, giraffe, rhinoceros and many other animals."
> http://www.alshindagah.com/Shindagah75/a_peak_into_the_past.htm

Is there evidence of human occupation? Despite its significance as a bridge between Africa and Eurasia, surprisingly very little is known about Arabia's early prehistory. This part of the world has been largely ignored by European scholars, mainly due to the inhospitable terrain. Fortunately, though, Saudi-sponsored archaeologists have been doing a little digging.

> "Humans have inhabited the Arabian Desert since early Pleistocene times (i.e., about 2.6 million years ago). Artifacts have been found widely, including at Neolithic sites in Qatar and Dubai, but are most abundant in the southwestern Rub' al-Khali. Archaeological research sponsored by the Saudi government has uncovered many Paleolithic sites. Remains of cultures from the past 3,000 years occur in many parts of the peninsula."
> (Source: britannica.com)

"The first concrete evidence of human presence in the Arabian Peninsula dates back 15,000 to 20,000 years. Bands of hunter-gatherers roamed the land, living off wild animals and plants. As the European ice cap melted during the last Ice Age, some 15,000 years ago, the climate in the peninsula became dry. Vast plains once covered with lush grasslands gave way to scrubland and deserts, and wild animals vanished. River systems also disappeared, leaving in their wake the dry river beds (wadis) that are found in the peninsula today."

http://www.saudiembassy.net/about/country-information/history.aspx

The dates given above (i.e. Late Miocene, Pleistocene, 15,000–20,000 years ago, etc.) are vague and contradictory; more importantly, there is no taking into account of the recent evidence showing how neighbouring North Africa underwent a catastrophic "climate change" in a geological blink of an eye. Are we to believe the Arabian Desert didn't suffer a similar fate at the same time as the Sahara? Sounds highly unlikely, especially when taking into account how both deserts lie on the same latitude – they are right next to each other and the only thing that separates them is the Red Sea, so how is this possible? Even if we invoke the consensus view that a change in the Earth's orbit (Milankovitch cycles?) was responsible for the Sahara's cataclysmic transformation, it stands to good reason, given the close proximity of the two deserts, that both areas must have "choked" up with sand around the same time. We find support for this in an article titled "Sahara's Abrupt

Desertification Started By Changes In Earth's Orbit, Accelerated By Atmospheric and Vegetation Feedbacks," published in the American Geophysical Union (July 12, 1999): "One of the most striking climate changes of the past 11,000 years caused the abrupt desertification of the Saharan and Arabia regions midway through that period."

El-Baz also makes the obvious connection:

"In the past, hidden rivers have proved a source of water. Dr. El-Baz pointed out that this could be the case in Saudi Arabia. He believes such rivers were formed during a relatively moist epoch that ended 5,000 years ago after enduring for 6,000 years." http://www.nytimes.com/1993/03/30/science/ science-watch-signs-of-ancient-river.html

In the same article, El-Baz, in believing he has discovered a very large paleo-river (he's dubbed it the "Kuwait River") under the sands of Arabia has this to say: "Since thriving civilizations existed along the Nile, Tigris and Euphrates when the hypothesized river flowed, it too may have supported civilizations and may produce some archaeological remains."

It is very apparent the Sahara and Arabian deserts were once co-existing sub-tropical paradises – lush green savannahs supporting a wide variety of life, including a large human population. Thousands of people once dwelt there – hunting, fishing and farming the land. That is until about 5,000 years ago, when something catastrophic occurred, resulting in both regions becoming choked by sand. By way of prophetic support, I would offer the following.

Although evidence for human occupation (artefacts) exists in Arabia, unlike the thousands of graves in the Sahara, to date no human remains have been found. However, the more recent awareness of Arabia's ancient watercourses has prompted a new research project (a five-year project) to get underway. The European Research Council has funded (€2.34 million) a University of Oxford-led investigation into human evolution in which a multidisciplinary research team will look at how long-term climate change affected early humans and animals in the region (Phys.org May 1, 2012). I predict that archaeologists will find many similarities with the lost Saharan water world, including that of human remains, graves and rock art. Time will tell.

Where did all the sand in Arabia come from?

The enormous Rub' al-Khali is also known as the Empty Quarter for good reason: it is one of the most inhospitable places in the world with extreme aridity and intense temperatures (summers typically stay above 50 degrees Celsius). At 650,000 square kilometres it has an area exceeding that of France. The sand overlies gravel or gypsum and the dunes reach heights of up to 250 metres. The sands consist of 80 to 90 percent quartz with the remainder feldspar, whose iron oxide-coated grains colour the sands orange and red. The question is: where did such immense amounts of sand come from? As with the Sahara, the source of the sand remains a matter of conjecture:

Rub' al-Khali, (Empty Quarter) one of the world's largest continuous bodies of sand in the world. The result of millions of years of erosion and deposition or are we looking at a much more recent extraterrestrial 'accretion' event?

Source: Wikimedia Commons

> "Very little evidence regarding the age and origin of the sand seas can be found within the sand seas themselves. [...] In light of this long erosional interval, it is difficult to determine when the first sand seas began to form."
> http://pubs.usgs.gov/of/1983/0749/report.pdf

It could not have been sourced locally as almost all the surrounding outcrops are carbonates. This has led some to search further afield:

"Surrounded by carbonate outcrops, the source of the desert's siliceous sediment (quartz sand) is disputed among scientists, though most of it seems to have been eroded from the Zagros Mountains in Iran and the highlands in the Arabian Peninsula. The age of the Rub' al-Khali dunes is also disputed."[Author's parentheses]
http://ismanual.voices.wooster.edu/files/2012/12/Dan.pdf

It is difficult to see how the Zagros Mountains play a part here, as they are composed primarily of limestone and shale (Encyclopedia Britannica).

In contrast, El-Baz (personal email) believes that the Arabian sand owes its origin to the same source as the Sahara: the underlying Nubian Sandstone (of Cretaceous age), which also abounds in the eastern part of the Arabian Peninsula. However, unlike his work on the Sahara, El-Baz presents no model as too how the Arabian sand settled into its present location. One would imagine El-Baz would adopt a similar fluvial model to that of the Sahara.

Others have proposed that many recycling events over millions of years have created the sand. Either way there is little to be gained by discussing the merits of each individual theory, for it is abundantly clear no one theory prevails and the fact is the provenance of the Arabian sand as with the Sahara remains unknown – we have another colossal body of sand of unconfirmed origin. That being said, one thing scholars do tend to agree on (and promote with religious fervour) is that sand takes millions of years to form and the dunes we see today have pretty much been in place for tens of thousands of years. With this in mind, we naturally recall the same basic "timescale" questions asked in regard to the Sahara. Such as, how could a thriving ecosystem exist in Arabia if so much sand was around? How did the rivers, lakes and tributaries flow? Did the sand in some way momentarily disappear allowing for a flourishing wet episode, which in turn came to a catastrophic end as the sand magically reappeared? Impossible! The timescale doesn't allow, so round and round we go again. There is little doubt that the Arabian sand could not have been around in the volumes seen today, as it would have been inconsistent with the idyllic subtropical paradise that once existed here.

What of the sand throughout the globe?

Map showing some of the world's major deserts.
Background map credit:Vvb83 on fi.wikipedia

The last two chapters have been devoted to calling into question the consensus view as to the origin of two of the largest accumulations of dune sand on the planet, the Sahara and Arabian deserts. The question that naturally follows, is what about the other quartz-rich deserts of the world, such as the Namib in Southern Africa, the Gobi in China, the Thar in India, and the great sandy deserts of Australia? All comprise colossal amounts of sand – where did it all come from? In addition, what of the world's quartz-rich beaches and vast sandstone deposits such as those seen in the Grand Canyon, and what of the lesser-known underlying Nubian Sandstone? The fact is that quartz sand is anywhere and everywhere imaginable on Earth (sand dunes exist even in Antarctica!). The question is: where did it originate?

The western state of Rajasthan hosts the large Thar Desert in Northern India.

Credit: sushmita balasubramani.

GRANITE – THE PRIMARY SOURCE OF QUARTZ SAND… OR IS IT?

All scholars hold the view that the *primary* source of the world's quartzose sand and sandstone deposits is granite rock – that is to say billions of years of weathering and erosion of granite outcrops created the sand that forms our beaches, sandy deserts and sandstone deposits globally. It is believed some deposits may have undergone multiple recycling events – i.e. sand to sandstone, to sand and round again – as some propose occurred with the aforementioned deserts. But ultimately the origin of all quartz grains lies with granite rock. But is this correct? Or could there be an alternative explanation to this seemingly impregnable bastion of uniformitarianism?

"Rock of ages"

"Granite is a common type of felsic intrusive igneous rock that is granular and phaneritic in texture. Granites can be predominantly white, pink, or gray in colour, depending on their mineralogy. The word 'granite' comes from the Latin granum, a grain, in reference to the coarse-grained structure of such a holocrystalline rock.

The grains are large enough to be visible with the unaided eye. By definition, granite is an igneous rock with at least 20% quartz and up to 65% alkali feldspar by volume."
(Granite Wiki)

Feldspars are a family of silicate minerals that occur in igneous rocks. There are many different members to the feldspar group. Silicon and oxygen form the foundation for the group, but calcium, sodium and potassium are also present.

Granite rock: clusters of interlocking crystals can clearly be seen.

Source: Wikimedia Commons.

Granite is called the "rock of ages" for good reason – it is extremely hardwearing and as such a popular material for kitchen countertops, floor tiles, paving stones, curbing and stair treads. Because of its weather-resistant properties it is also used as decorative facings (veneer) on buildings and is the preferred material for cemetery monuments (gravestones etc.).

Geologists are firmly committed to the idea that quartz grains derive from granite. It is said that billions of years of water erosion washes away the feldspars to form clay – leaving behind the virtually insoluble quartz grains. In other words, to reduce granite down to its constituent quartz, a whopping 80 per cent of material has to be eroded away in solution. A process that as improbable as it sounds, also breaks up the quartz clusters into individual crystals and then coats them in a thin layer of iron oxide.

Quartz sand from granite rock.
Source: Author

The image above shows a piece of granite rock next to a measured pile of quartz beach sand. The sand represents 20 per cent the volume of the granite. The purpose of this image is to demonstrate just how much rock is required to produce a few kilograms of sand. Granite is a tough, hard rock and yet when weathered most of it turns to clay. When considering the primary origin of sand please bear this image in mind.

Eighty per cent is a very large portion of rock to remove and there is little doubt, that if correct, the process of filtering out quartz crystals would take billions of years even in exceptionally wet environments. Therefore, everything seems to be in order here, but what if we were to scale things up a little and 'reverse' the process so to speak?

For instance, take a look at any image of large sandy dunes (in this book or photos on the internet). Now imagine reinstating the 80 per cent of weathered material back to these dunes. As I'm sure you will agree, if sand owes its origin to granite rock then the source must have been truly gargantuan. In fact, it is difficult to conceive the amount of rock required to produce so much sand. Even if the volume of quartz is increased to 30 or 40 per cent (25 per cent is mentioned here: http://www2.nau.edu/~gaud/RiodeFlag/ignsrck.htm) the amount of basement rock required remains colossal.

Some rough area calculations will further our understanding of the tremendous scale involved. For example, Saharan sand covers an area of 2.5 million square kilometres. This would require a source rock spanning an incredible 12.5 million square kilometres (i.e. 2.5 million = one-fifth of original source, then multiplied by 5 = 12.5 million square kilometres). At one-fifth the volume, the vast oceans of sand bear no comparison to the colossal amount of "rock of ages" required. If the exercise were repeated with the Arabian Desert, which spans 650,000 square kilometres, another biblical granitic source spanning some 3.23 million square kilometreswould be needed. As with all the world's deserts for every dune field we have to add four times what we see to make "whole" again.

Consideration also has to be given to the world's abundant sandstone beds that cover Earth's crust. A prime example would be the sand comprising the Navajo Sandstone layer that is spread across the U.S. states of Northern Arizona, Northwestern Colorado, Nevada and Utah – outcropping in several regions mainly to the north of the Grand Canyon (notably Zion National Park).

Covering up to 400,000 square kilometres (an area the size of California) the Navajo Sandstone represents "one of the greatest accumulations of ancient dune sand in the world" (Chronic, 1983, p.260). It is comparable with the great ergs of the Sahara and the Rub' al Khai. Sometimes described as the world's deepest sandpile it is over 700 metres deep in places (Crawford, 1988, p.15). It consists of approximately 90 per cent quartz (some say more), around 5 per cent potassium feldspar, and 5 per cent clays and other accessory minerals.

According to truthbrigade.com (http://truthbrigade.com/ drlar/crystal/xls012.htm), the volume of the Navajo Sandstone is estimated to be over 40,000 cubic kilometres. This, however, fails to take into account differential compaction, eroded sections with missing tops where the original thickness is unknown, and "those areas/volumes on the margins of the basin which have been removed by erosion and/or involved in later mountain-building and, thus, are absent from the geological record". This has led some to suggest that the volume of sand deposited during the formation of the Navajo Sandstone was in excess of 100,000 cubic kilometres.

Stevens Arch, on the wall of the Escalante River Canyon near its junction with Coyote Gulch. The arch opening, formed in a layer of Navajo Sandstone, is estimated to be 220 feet wide and 160 feet high.

Source: Wikimedia Commons.

Truthbrigade.com further suggests that:

> "If this amount of sand was converted into a crude line of enormous piles, it would somewhat resemble from a distance and be volumetrically equivalent to the Colorado Rocky Mountains!"
> (ibid.)

As with all the world's sand deposits, what most people don't seem to consider here is the volume of granite rock required to produce so much quartz sand. Using the Rocky Mountains analogy above, we would require a granitic source five times the size of the Colorado Rockies just to produce the Navajo Sandstone deposit – staggering volumes of source rock would have to be eroded.

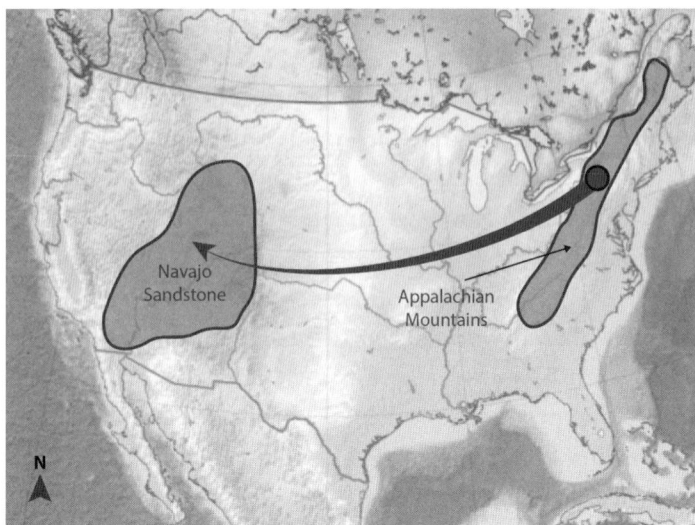

Left: The Approximate extent of the Navajo Erg. Right: The Appalachian mountain range, the apparent source of the sand which we will discuss shortly. The Navajo bed would have to be extended at least four times to gain an idea of the volume of rock required to create so much sand – this would equate to virtually one fifth of the USA for the Navajo deposit alone.

Source: Author

There are many other vast sandstone deposits comprising the Colorado Plateau, none more so than some of the layers that spectacularly line the walls of the Grand Canyon. The Coconino Sandstone (third layer from the top), for example, consists primarily of fine, well-sorted quartz grains (>95 per cent) and covers an area of at least 518,000 square kilometres (200,000 square miles). It is estimated to contain at least 41,700 cubic kilometres (10,000 cubic miles) of sand (A Reality Check on Flood Geology.

Timothy K. Helble.pdf). Where did this sand come from, and how do we know? This is roughly the volume of the lowest estimate for the Navajo Sandstone. Allowing for differential compaction, eroded sections, etc., as noted above, it's quite possible the Coconino Sandstone may have also originally been in the region of 100,000 cubic kilometres. Either way, just two deposits of sandstone and we're potentially looking for parent rock many times the size of the Rocky Mountains!

What of the other Grand Canyon quartz-rich sandstone layers, many of which also spread across several states or, as in the case of the Tapeats Sandstone, are believed to underlie the whole continent? If we adopt the consensus view of erosion from granite, they all require granite sources five times the volumes seen today. It begs the question, just how many Rocky ranges would it take to create so much sand, and moreover, where are they? Where's the evidence for the mass erosion of granite?

Grand Canyon National Park, North Rim in Arizona. Note the distinct sedimentary layers. Were they laid down in relatively rapid succession or over billions of years? If billions of years, then why virtually flat horizontal strata?

Source: Staplegunther at English Wikipedia

The same applies to Nubian Sandstone, the apparent source of the Sahara and Arabian sands. Having written to a few geologists I can reveal that no quantitative analysis of the Nubian Sandstone by area or volume has been done. Indeed, the impression is that nobody has even thought of asking the question let alone consulting any calculators. Which is a little perplexing for had they done so they would have realised there are some impossible numbers here. Fortunately, I have made some rough calculations.

According to Wikipedia: "The Nubian sandstone complex has a thickness varying from under 500 m to over 3000 meters" (Wikipedia).

"In Egypt, the strata of major hydrogeological interest are composed of a sandstone complex ranging from Cambrian to Upper Cretaceous in age. This sandstone complex, commonly known as the Nubian Sandstone, has a thickness varying from less than 500 m to more than 3000 m and rests directly on Precambrian basement."

(http://qjegh.geoscienceworld.org/content/15/2/127. abstract)

"Nubian (Jurassic to late Cretaceous): Egypt Sudan, Libya, and Chad, and part of Asia Minor. First recognised in 1947 as the "Nubia," this thick widespread (1000 to 3000 m) sandstone sequence contains but minor shales. Alluvial, coastal plain, and marine shelf environments."

(Pettijohn, 1987. Sand and Sandstone, p 6).

Some have also proposed it attains a thickness of more than 3,500 metres in the northern localities of the Dakhla Basin and over 4,500 in the north-western part (Hermina 1990; Klitzsch and Wycisk 1999). This gives a good idea of thickness but what of the area covered?

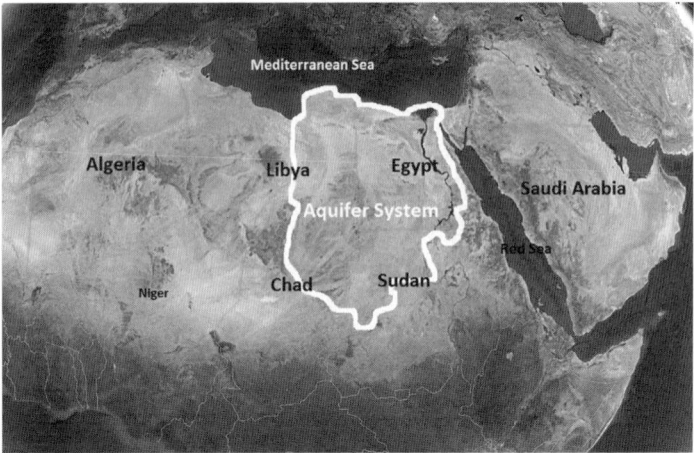

The highlighted area shows the Nubian Sandstone Nubian Sandstone Aquifer System (NSAS), which straddles four countries. The 'Nubia' actually underlies a far greater area than that shown.

Source: Wiki.

As we have seen, the Nubian Sandstone Aquifer System (NSAS) is called thus because it is comprised of Nubian Sandstone. It covers a land area spanning just over two million square kilometres. But this is just Northeast Africa; the "Nubia" also underlies large parts of the Arabian Peninsula, stretching as far as Israel and Jordan (outcropping spectacularly in both). With this in mind, I believe we could easily double this figure to 4,000,000 square kilometres. Now, if we take an average thickness of 2,000 metres and multiply this by four million, this would give us 8,000,000 cubic kilometres of sand – and even more staggering, a required source rock to the tune of an incredible 40,000,000 cubic kilometres. To repeat, a granitic source of some *40,000,000 cubic kilometres* would be required to create the "Nubia". This would equate to roughly four hundred times the Rockies! It is without doubt that Nubian Sandstone is the largest sand deposit in the entire world by far. Who knows, probably the largest sand deposit in the solar system?

There are, of course, other substantial sandstone deposits around the world (nowhere even close to the "Nubia" though) such as those that occur in Niger, Kazakhstan, Uzbekistan, Gabon (Franceville Basin) and South Africa (Karoo Basin), plus many, many more. Indeed, since sandstone makes up roughly 25 per cent of all sedimentary rocks, and as sedimentary rocks cover 75 per cent of the Earth's surface, there are too many to mention.

And then there are the deposits of quartz-rich sand that form the world's beaches (not to mention the abundant sources of mobile sand on the seafloor). Some brief examples are Cassino Beach in Brazil, which stretches for over 150 miles (241 kilometres) in length, and Cox's Bazar, Bangladesh, which is known as the world's longest "natural sand" beach and also stretches over 150 miles. Then there's Padre Island, Texas, U.S. (130 miles long), Ninety Mile Beach, New Zealand (the clue is in the name) and Playa Novillero, Mexico (90 kilometres). And also Virginia Beach, Virginia, U.S. (35 miles long), Long Beach in Washington, U.S. (30 miles), Stockton Beach in Australia (20 miles), and many, many more. Although quantities are unknown, it is visibly obvious almost all hold (small allowance for volcanic and shells beaches) vast quantities of quartz-rich sand. As mentioned above, for every beach and every dune we have to add four times what is seen to gain an idea of the size of the parent rock required.

Incidentally, it is estimated that at least 70 per cent of the world's sandy beaches are currently eroding (Dickson, 2010) and we are often presented with press releases to the effect of "beaches are running out of sand" and "beaches and coastlines eroding away". Why is that? Could the source of sand have dried up? If not, how were the beaches allowed to form in the first place? Why isn't the erosion rate of granite (or quartz rocks in general) keeping pace with the erosion of the beaches? Has a state of equilibrium been interrupted, or is it possible that some of the world's beaches (and coastlines) are eroding away because they were only formed a few thousand years ago? Shouldn't the erosion of coastlines (and sandstones, granites) actually create more sand?

Cassino Beach – Rio Grande, Brazil. Consider the possibility that sand fell into the oceans and washed ashore… and this is what forms our beaches?

Source: tribalingua.wordpress.com.

Although not an exact science, the above gives the reader a good idea of the tremendous scale involved. We can further this by asking: is it possible to calculate the total volume of sand in the whole world? As it happens, some rough calculations have been done: "There are approximately 200 million cubic kilometers of continental sediments. Assuming that about a fourth of it is sand, the total volume of sand is perhaps 50 million cubic kilometers." (http://www.sandatlas. org/2011/11/brain-games-with-sand-grains/)

The above-quoted quantity would cover the earth to a depth of approximately 98 metres. However, if raised on the continental blocks (where most sand is concentrated) a height of 333 metres would be realised. This is very conservative estimate as some (Horn and Adams) have proposed a much higher number of 522 million cubic kilometres for the continental sediments with a third of it being sand (Pettijohn, 1987, *Sand and Sandstone*, p.5). On the continents this would equate to a height of 1,160 metres (approx. 1.16 kilometres). Mind-blowing quantities?! Maybe, but we've yet to reinstate the 80 per cent of eroded rock. Doing this would give us a staggering 5,800 metres (19,160 feet) or, close to six kilometres of granite rock towering over Earth's land area! To say we are looking for granite sources on a planetary-wide scale here would be an understatement. Was there ever enough granite to produce so much sand or are we looking at such impossible volumes that we need to look elsewhere for answers, extraterrestrial sources perhaps?

IN SEARCH OF GRANITE SOURCES

Most introductory geology textbooks report that Earth's outer layer is made of two grand categories of rocks: basaltic and granitic. Basaltic rocks underlie the seafloors and granitic rocks make up the continents. Granite is an intrusive igneous rock (plutonic) – a liquid rock (magma) that formed under Earth's surface by slowly pushing up to fill any cracks or spaces it can find, sometimes pushing existing rock out of the way (hence "intrusive"), a process that can take millions of years (according to the consensus view). The large mineral crystals in granite are evidence that it cooled slowly from molten rock material beneath Earth's surface.

Granite often occurs as relatively small, less than 100 square kilometres of stock masses (stocks) and in batholiths (larger than 100 square kilometres) that are often associated with orogenic mountain ranges. Although the most abundant rock in the continental crust, granite is largely overlaid by sedimentary rock and other material. There is only one way that granite becomes exposed on the surface of Earth and that is when uplifted from a depth (usually from about 1 to 20 miles down) with overlying sedimentary rocks eroding away.

Granite outcrops that occur around the world are typically found in the eroded remnants of ancient mountain ranges such as the Appalachian Mountains in North America (which we will discuss shortly) and the mountains of Scotland and Scandinavia. Past glacial action is also believed to be a contributing factor in exposing granite intrusions on ancient mountain ranges (e.g. in New England, U.S. and Scandinavia) and in combination with major tectonic uplifts, such as in the Sierra Nevada of California, the European Alps and the Andes mountains of South America.

Half Dome, Yosemite, a classic granite dome of the Sierra Nevada Batholith. An apparent source of quartz grains?

Source: Wikimedia Commons.

Before any of the above was known early geologists naturally assumed the world's mountains held the key to the *primary* origin of all sand deposits – it seems obvious doesn't it? Those enormous pointy things that reach out and touch the sky must be the source. These geologists reasoned that the process of physical and chemical weathering broke apart the rocks and gravity transported the sediments downslope over many billions of years (the rock cycle) – thus creating the world's quartz sand and vast sandstone deposits. We now know this to be incorrect as the majority of mountain ranges are not only made up of the wrong material but they are also too young, having only formed in the last few hundred million years. Examples would include the relatively young Himalayas, the Alps and the Andes – they are composed *largely* of sedimentary rocks including sandstones, shale and mudstone, and thus cannot be considered the primary source of such extensive volumes of quartz sand.

Unfortunately, geologists today are still making the same blinkered mistake – with little or no research they are nominating the nearest mountain range or largest outcrop as being the source for most deposits and if these are found to be made of the wrong stuff, they venture on to the next mountain range, and so on. The erroneous assumption that the central Saharan mountains were responsible for the Saharan sand would be a prime example.

The fact is that the provenance of quartz sand with respect to source determination is at best highly speculative, if not downright impossible:

"The question of provenance is one of the most difficult the sedimentary petrographer is called upon to solve. […] Although there may be differences in the statistical average for the several source rock types, it is commonly impossible to assign specific grains in a sandstone to one or another source."

(F. J. Pettijohn, 1987, Sand and Sandstone, pp. 255–6)

That being said, although the provenance, or source area, of the majority of sand accumulations worldwide (beach, dune, sandstone or otherwise) remains unknown (a situation that really shouldn't exist), some researchers believe they have found a link between certain deposits and their respective granitic sources. Let us take a look at a few.

Searching…

We recall one of the signature outcrops of the Colorado Plateau, the Navajo Sandstone which, as mentioned, spans 400,000 square kilometres across several U.S. states. The place from which all this quartz sand was eroded has long mystified geologists. In the early days it was assumed the nearby massive range of the Rocky Mountains were responsible (and many other sedimentary rock layers in the Colorado Plateau). However, more recent studies have shown the geology of the Rocky Mountains bears little resemblance to the Navajo sand, so it is now accepted that any local source has to be all but ruled out. This has caused geologists to look further afield, and when I say further afield, I mean the other side of the U.S!

The Appalachian Mountains

The Appalachian Mountains are a chain of mountains located in the eastern United States and Canada, running across the North American continent from Alabama in the south to Newfoundland in the north. The mountain range measures roughly 100 to 300 miles (160.9 to 482.7 kilometres) wide and covers an area of about 1,500 miles (2,413.5 kilometres) from north to south (image below). In 2003, geologist Jeffrey Rahl and his colleagues analysed tiny grains of the mineral zircon embedded in the Navajo Sandstone. By "dating" these zircon grains using the uranium-lead (U-Pb) radioactive method, it has been postulated that the sand grains in the Navajo Sandstone came from the Appalachians far to the east. If this is true, it means the sand grains were transported at least 1,250 miles (2,012 kilometres) across North America.

I refer the reader to the image on page 54 showing the Navajo deposit with the respect to the proposed source, the Appalachians in the east. How does 100,000 cubic kilometres of quartz sand become transported over such a vast distance? In a very vague and feeble attempt to explain, geologists here propose an immense transcontinental "river system" delivered the sand to the west where the wind took over and swept it into a fantastic sand pile (http://www.agiweb.org/geotimes/nov03/NN_navajo.html).

Considering that Navajo Sandstone is believed to be some 180 million years old and was built layer by layer over 15 million years, you would need more than a leap of faith to accept this. It is not only impossible for such a river to have persisted for millions of years but also inconceivable that it would create such a virtually pure deposit of quartz sand (90 per cent) hundreds of feet thick and covering thousands of square miles. Modern rivers such as the Mississippi, Nile and Amazon do not do this.

If such a river did exist, where was it? Certainly nowhere near the surface as there are no geological features to suggest a great transcontinental river once flowed across the U.S. Perhaps the evidence lies hidden below ground? We recall the network of paleo-rivers and tributaries hidden beneath the Sahara and Arabian deserts, which are thought to be around 20 to 30 million years old. Indeed, even more so in that, to transport so much sand over such a long period of time and over such a great distance, this river must have been truly colossal – is there any evidence for a great "radar" river system? The author is unaware of any ground-penetrating radar evidence for a continent wide paleo-river and would suggest with a great deal of confidence that none will ever be found. It would seem unlikely that the Navajo sand sea and its proposed parent source, the river system, has magically disappeared off the face of the Earth.

It's not just the sand. We also have to take into account the clay-forming feldspars which, having eroded from the Appalachians, would equate to roughly four times the volume of sand (approximately 500,000 cubic kilometres). Added to this the majority of Colorado Plateau sandstones (and corresponding four times silt), which some also believe originated from the Appalachians, and we have mind-boggling quantities of material that was apparently transported across the US.

Few rivers in the world are over 2,000 kilometres long. Even if they were, it would be highly unlikely these rivers could move such vast quantities of sediment that distance. Modern rivers do carry heavy sediment loads, but they do not move quartz-bearing sediments over such distances in the suggested quantities.

The proposed "river system" must have been an interior one, that is to say, it didn't flow out to sea. A logical assumption since the Navajo Sandstone wouldn't be where it is today if it was initially washed out to the ocean. This raises the question as to where the many millions of tons of eroded sediment forming silt ended up (the by-product of any quartz sand production). At a rough estimate, this would be some ten times the volume of Navajo sand, enough perhaps to cover the whole U.S. at some considerable depth. Where did this settle?

One would naturally assume it was deposited in the same rough location as the Navajo Sandstone to form multiple sedimentary deposits of shale (or mudstone and suchlike) the most common of sedimentary rock – is this what happened? Unfortunately, there's no mention of this by geologists; as discussed previously, the awkward question as to the whereabouts of the weathered material (clays) from granite is rarely considered or simply dismissed as transported "in solution" somewhere.

But it must have settled somewhere and by all accounts it should be a more prominent geological feature than all the sandstone deposits put together! Perhaps it underwent a few recycling events and was scattered throughout the region to form some of the sedimentary layers we see outcropping in locations such as the Grand Canyon? There are plenty of shale deposits in the region. However, as we are dealing with gargantuan volumes on a continent-wide scale, the evidence here should be unequivocal with large-scale deposits consistent with that of being transported across the U.S. and laid down in one location. After all, this is the same sediment that apparently produced the Navajo (and many other sandstone deposits such as the Coconino), which not only managed to remain as virtually "pure" quartz but was also deposited in one basic location, despite supposedly being laid down over many millions of years.

No matter how you look this, evidence for Appalachian silt the other side of the continent should be glaringly obvious, as clear and as distinctive as its derivative, the Navajo sand bed and other quartzose deposits. Geologists should be confidently identifying such deposits and explaining how they got there. But they cannot. A question for geologists: how is it that only the quartz ended up being deposited as the Navajo and Coconino Sandstones? What happened to all the feldspars and mica?

The Appalachian Mountains are rolling, green mountains and look nothing like the Rockies or the Tetons. When compared with the snow-capped peaks of the Himalayas, Andes or Alps they are seldom mentioned among the world's great mountain ranges, mainly because they consist mostly of low gentle ridges, almost like the keel of a boat. The Appalachians are a complex mix of mountains and have a long and complex geologic history spanning some 480 million years.

A look at rocks exposed in today's Appalachian Mountains reveals elongated belts of folded and thrust-faulted marine sedimentary rocks, volcanic rocks and slivers of ancient ocean floor. So here we see they are largely of the wrong composition.

Thought to have formed as a result of a series of continental collisions, granitic outcrops occur in several areas, especially in the Piedmont region. They vary tremendously in size, shape and position in the landscape. Some consist of small, flat-lying exposures (or flatrocks) only a few square feet in area while others span between a few hundred square kilometres to approximately 2,000 square kilometres, as is the case with the Rolesville granite batholith located in North Carolina. One way of visualising the granitic intrusions would be to describe the Appalachians as an elongated bowl of porridge with prunes protruding the surface – as the granitic outcrops are just that, rock intrusions.

Diagram showing granitic outcrops in the Piedmont region of the Appalachians. Despite being surrounded by thick sedimentary rock it is said these plutons contributed to the Coconino and Navajo sand deposits the other side of the US! Does it make sense? Were they ever once large enough to supply biblical proportions of pure quartz sand?

Source: I Marine & H Bledsoe.

Although there is little information on this (no one, it seems is too interested in tracking down the primary source of sand), a conservative estimate of the total area covered by granitic outcrops found in the Appalachians would be about 3 per cent. This would equate to roughly 36,000 square kilometres of granitic outcrops, if that. Was this ever enough to produce the huge sandstone deposits in the western U.S.? I strongly doubt this for several reasons.

Using our height formula and bearing in mind the weathered material, some absolutely impossible heights would have to be realised. Indeed, today's granitic outcrops would once have had to stand at an incredible 28 kilometres to create the Navajo and Coconino deposits alone. This is some three times the height of the Himalayas and sounds highly implausible – especially when taking into account the fact that granite is an intrusive rock not a sedimentary rock. It forms under Earth's surface (mainly sedimentary rock overlain with soil) which having eroded away exposes the granitic rock. This deems the whole of the Appalachian complex must have once stood even higher than its granitic intrusions. Although the Appalachians are vast in length, peaking at a mere 6,684 feet (2,037 metres) they are low lying, and while there is ample evidence to suggest they were higher in the past, I doubt any geologist would ever suggest they reached the dizzying heights of 28 kilometres. This would give unprecedented heights as well as unfathomable quantities of sediments, bordering on biblical proportions.

Some may postulate that the Appalachians underwent several phases of tectonic uplift (mountain forming) and erosion simultaneously, that is to say several kilometres of rock were eroded away at the same time as the mountains were slowly thrust upwards, thus preventing them from ever attaining such astronomical heights. This is a nonstarter, inasmuch as the granite outcrops are said to have formed around 300 million years ago while the Navajo Sandstone is reputedly about 180 million years old. What this means is the granitic intrusions seen today are the only possible source for the sand. But this makes little sense, for it is impossible for them to have stood at 28 kilometres high – as rock intrusions that began life just below Earth's surface they cannot be too far off from where they stand today. This is proven by the fact that sedimentary rocks weather much faster than granitic rock. So, if the granites were at any considerable elevation, the surrounding sedimentary material would have weathered away first, leaving behind some truly imposing granite prunes! Like skyscrapers piercing the skies of the world's major cities, they would have dwarfed the surrounding landscape. Nowhere on Earth has this occurred on such a scale and it certainly isn't a feature of the Appalachians.

If we assume for a moment that the sand did somehow originate from the Appalachians, then exactly how would this work? To understand this further let us briefly run through the likely sequence of events before analysing the main points a little more in depth. As will become evident, the whole scenario is impossible. I would add, what follows here could also apply to the process of quartz production worldwide.

The process would go something like this; rains fall on the mountains and over eons of time erosion removes thousands of feet of overlying mainly sedimentary rock, exposing the more resistant bodies of granite. The surrounding rocks along with the bulk (80 per cent) of the granitic rocks weather away into solution to form silt and clay minerals (mud). These would normally be washed out to sea by rivers, but as we are dealing with an interior river system, they are transported and deposited at some, yet to be found, location in the west. We can only assume a basin containing a lake here. The tough quartz crystals on the other hand are not suspended in solution; they are transported along rivers beds by a process called saltation (jumping along the bed of a river). Regardless, they combine to form unfathomable volumes of clay, silt and sand (mud) which would have been deposited in and around said lake, in particular around the mouth of the river feeding it.

Incessant rain?

It is without doubt that the erosion, transportation and deposition of millions of tons of sediment thousands of miles west across the continent via a river system involved rain, and lots of it. In fact, rainwater must have been continuous and totally unremitting for literally billions of years in order to create so much sand. If there were any significant respite then the sand/silt/mud would have been more randomly scattered, i.e. deposited further upstream during dryer periods, thus more prone to wind transportation and deposition. In essence, it wouldn't have ended up in one basic place.

In any case, there is no evidence whatsoever for a great east–west continental river system emanating from the direction of the Appalachians and depositing sediments en route. This raises the question of: what changed if the Appalachians were responsible for the majority of the sedimentary layers in the west? What great cataclysm befell the U.S. causing a giant east–west river system to disappear off the face of the earth?

Where were the Milankovitch cycles (MCs) during all this time?

As we have seen, many believe the MCs were the driving force in shaping the climate of North Africa (Arabia etc.), i.e. causing the region to experience cyclical wet and dry periods over many millennia – are we to believe the same variations in Earth's axial tilt played no recognisable part in the U.S.? Where were the cycles during the erosion, transportation and deposition of unfathomable quantities of sedimentary material apparently laid down in the west? Are the MCs recorded in the Navajo or Coconino sandstone layers? Are any of them recorded in the strata of the Grand Canyon? If not, why not? Were these regions exempt from global changes? If the MCs were responsible for the catastrophic transformation of North Africa, the Middle East and the Asian continent then why can't scholars correlate these events with events in the U.S.? It's all very vague and riddled with inconsistencies – yet more reasons to dismiss the Milankovitch cycles as they clearly do not work.

Magical filtration system?

As we can see, the deposition of several million tons of sediment in the west also involved mud (clay, silt and sand), and lots of it. In fact, it's difficult to conceive the quantities of mud involved – probably enough to turn Earth into one gigantic mud ball. It's a wonder this alone didn't silt up the whole system. Mixed in with this mud we have the relatively small amount of quartz grains, at a guess probably less than 2 per cent (if that, when taking into account the additional mix of eroded material from the Appalachians, i.e. soil etc.). Laid down in a continental basin or lake somewhere to form multiple beds of sediment, how on Earth was this filtered out to form the vast *pure* sandstone deposits found in the Colorado Plateau? The Navajo sand sea comprises of more than 90 per cent pure quartz sand, and the Coconino an even higher concentration. Both deposits stretch for thousands of miles – what magical filtration system manages to sort hundreds of thousands of cubic kilometres of quartz grains from masses upon masses of silt and clay? Just how did the quartz sand end up so well sorted? If of the same origin, why the variants in the purity of the sand? Are similar processes at work today? Are the Appalachian granites still churning out first-phase quartz grains creating new, virtually *pure* sand seas at some location? If so, where? If not, why not?

We may ask the same questions in regard to the world's granitic outcrops: are they still giving up their 20 per cent quartz? Mainstream says yes but since we are dealing with erosional processes that take millions upon millions of years, it is imperceptible on such a small scale. Indeed!

While it isn't doubted that quartz grains are being eroded from granitic rocks, I would suggest this to be on such a negligible scale as to be virtually *ineffective*. Certainly not even coming close to ever providing a source for the world's vast deposits of quartz sand (be it beach, dune, sandstone or otherwise) no matter how much time you ascribe to it. Time just doesn't favour the laying down of vast pure deposits of sand (first phase or recycled). It would require the supposition that there was no environmental or geological change during the multimillion years of deposition – given the dynamicity of Earth, highly unlikely. Where were the Milankovitch cycles during such times? Why aren't glacial–interglacial periods clearly represented in the strata?

Rivers do of course carry sediments; some such as the Amazon, Mississippi, Nile and Indus carry very heavy loads. This is deposited at the mouth of the rivers to form new land called deltas. A prime example would be the Mississippi, which drains all or part of thirty-one U.S. states and two Canadian provinces between the Rocky and Appalachian Mountains, dumping the sediment in the Gulf of Mexico, forming a large soil-rich delta. As we have seen, sediment typically consists of sand, silt and clay. However, proportions can vary considerably between rivers. For instance, there is ample evidence to show that the Mississippi has not only deposited large amounts of sand in the past but this is an on-going process – so much so it has to be dredged on a regular basis to keep waterways open. But how much of river sand is quartz grains disintegrated from granitic outcrops? How much of this is primary source sand?

Using the standard model of granite taking many millions of years to erode it is logical to conclude this to be negligible – virtually undetectable. But if this so, then where does all the sand in our rivers come from if not source rock? It is thought that the majority of sand in rivers is derived from secondary sources (recycled) such as sandstone or unconsolidated sand washed down off the land – very little sand originates directly from granitic sources. This is easily understood when considering the slow erosion of granite rock versus the more rapid erosion of sedimentary rocks. And yet, it is from this "trickle" that the world's beaches were apparently formed; it is from this trickle that great oceans of dune sands are believed to have been created; it is from this trickle that enough sand to cover the continents to a height of 1,160 metres (approx. 1.16 kilometres) was created (eroded from rock that would stand at a height of 6 kilometres). Hard to believe given the fact that all the water, in all of the streams and rivers of the world represents only 0.005 per cent of all the water in the world outside the ocean basin.

When taking into account the above, it is plain to see there is something seriously wrong with the idea that vast swathes of sand (and sediment) were transported across the U.S. and dumped in the west via a river system. As demonstrated, there is no geological evidence whatsoever to support this.

The only thing linking the two is an apparent match between zircon crystals – nothing else! What does this tell us? It tells us that the dating of zircon grains is seriously flawed and cannot be relied on. Moreover, we are left with even more vast quartz sand seas of *unknown* origin.

NAMIB DESERT SAND PROVENANCE

As we have seen, there are many erroneous assumptions in regard to the origin and provenance of sand or as in the case of the Colorado sediments – science that just doesn't add up. Another example of where things just don't ring true concerns the origin of the Namib Desert of southern Africa.

> "The vast Namib Sand Sea, which covers roughly 13,125 square miles (34,000 square kilometers) along the coast of Namibia, is one of the world's oldest and largest sand deserts. However, little is known about the origin of its sands — whether they come from remote sources or local sediments. This uncertainty holds true with other large deserts as well, largely because one sand dune looks much like another."
> http://www.livescience.com/8889-sand-grains-african-desert-1-million-years.html

Using the same zircon U–Pb provenance method as above, a recent study has suggested that although the underlying Tsondab Sandstone may provide a source, the Orange River is the predominant ultimate source of sand for the Namib Desert dunes.

"We use UPb geochronology of detrital zircons to show that the primary source of sand is the Orange River at the southern edge of the Namib desert. Our burial ages obtained from measurments of the cosmogenic nuclides Be, Al and Ne suggest that the residence time of sand within the sand sea is at least one million years. We therefore conclude that, despite large climatic changes in the Namib region associated with Quaternary glacialinterglacial cycles, the area currently occupied by the Namib Sand Sea has never been entirely devoid of sand during the past million years."

http://www.ucl.ac.uk/~ucfbpvc/papers/ VermeeschNatGeo2010/

The sand begins its watery journey upstream before eventually settling along the coast to form dunes reaching heights of 60 to 240 metres (200 to 800 feet).

"After long-distance fluvial transport, Orange sand is washed by ocean waves and dragged northward by vigorous longshore currents. Under the incessant action of southerly winds, sand is blown inland and carried farther north to accumulate in the Namib erg, a peculiar wind-dominated sediment sink displaced hundreds of kilometres away from the river mouth. And yet changes in sand mineralogy along the way are minor."

http://eprints.bbk.ac.uk/4617/

Although the above suggests the sand has been in place for at least a million years, the Namib is reputed to be one of the oldest deserts in the world – a quick internet search will reveal ages of between 104 to 55 million years down to a possible maximum age of 5 to 6 million years. In other words, think of a number and add enough zeros so as to keep uniformitarian minds happy. The mind boggles as to how these figures were arrived at from a blanket of sand that looks as though it was laid down yesterday.

Namib Desert. Imagine reinstating the weathered feldspar material to the dunes above – it would equate to roughly five times the volume seen here. Even if the quartz content was considerably higher we are still looking at unimaginable volumes.

Source: Robur.q Wikimedia.

Where's the eroded material required to produce so much sand? Imagine reinstating it. The granitic source for such quantities must have been truly colossal and it is doubtful that even 100 million years would ever be enough time to create so much sand. If so, this would mean the Orange River must have remained virtually unaltered for the same length of time. This is highly unlikely when considering how this would incorporate the Miocene age (23 to 5.3 million years ago); marked by the drift of continents to their present position. We may ask how a river that apparently created the oldest desert in the world still survives while the river system that reputedly carried incomprehensible volumes of sediment across the U.S. has completely disappeared! What of sea-level fluctuations brought about by glacial-interglacial cycles or otherwise? As a massive coastal desert, surely they played a part? It would seem not.

"Despite large climatic changes in the Namib region associated with Quaternary glacial interglacial cycles, the area currently occupied by the Namib Sand Sea has never been entirely devoid of sand during the past million years."
http://eprints.bbk.ac.uk/4617/

The above speaks volumes for it reveals that authors are struggling with how "glacial-interglacial cycles" (MCs) seem to have had no effect on the accumulation of sand, and by extension the Orange River. Such concerns are understandable, as the whole thing sounds highly implausible.

I am reminded of how storms in 2014 uncovered a huge forest offshore from Borth in Wales – the stumps of hundreds of trees were exposed. This is actually a well-known phenomenon around the coasts of Britain and Ireland and mostly it reflects inroads by the sea as a result of rising sea levels after the last ice age some 5,000 years ago. Another forest was uncovered in Suffolk and another off Cornwall, and over the years this has happened on countless recorded occasions (and presumably on even more unrecorded occasions). Essentially, it reflects the drowning of the continental shelf around Britain and Ireland – including the drowning of the North Sea basin. Storms in the U.S. have also uncovered an ancient underwater forest off Alabama. The forest was apparently buried under a thick layer of sand for eons until it was uncovered by giant waves during Hurricane Katrina. Some of the pieces still had bark on them. It apparently provides evidence that coastal Alabama has risen between 60 and 120 feet in the last 50,000 years.

In addition to this, there is a wealth of human history lying submerged in ancient cities at the bottoms of the lakes, seas and oceans of the world. A few examples would include Herakleion and Eastern Canopus, Egypt; Port Royal, Jamaica; Atlit-Yam, Israel; and Pavlopetri in Greece. The point here is that some relatively recent climatic or geological events caused the above to become submerged – and yet deserts such as the Namib and its source, the Orange River, apparently remained unaffected for many millions of years.

The Orange River and its tributaries start close to the east coast and flow right across the continent and into the Atlantic.

Along the way the river picks up sand from a variety of rocks including sandstone and granite as well as kimberlite pipes with diamonds in them (C. Bristow, private email 2014). What this means is, apart from where the river channels though a narrow granite gorge at Augrabies, there is little in the way of a granitic source – certainly nothing resembling the vast granitic outcrops required to create the Namib sand sea. For this reason, most support the idea that the majority of sand originates from reworked sources, mainly sandstone – but, as we shall see, even this has its problems.

Composition

Sand collected from the Namib dunes (Sossus formation) showed the sand to be composed of about 46 per cent quartz, 24 per cent feldspar, 13 per cent rock fragments and 12 per cent heavy minerals (Low depositional porosity in aeolian sands and sandstones, Namib Desert, Dickinson & Ward 1993). The question is an obvious one: why is the feldspar content so high and the percentage of quartz so low if born from water?

Geology 101 deems that when granite becomes weathered the feldspars dissolve in solution to become clays, essentially leaving behind the more weather-resistant quartz grains – the primary source of dune sand, beaches and sandstone, or so we are taught – but the Sossus samples clearly don't support this. The feldspar content is far too high when considering their long-distance fluvial transport. How is this possible?

Sediment is washed down the Orange River for thousands of miles, it flows into the Atlantic where it is subjected to rough seas and fierce southerly winds which drives the sand hundreds of miles north up the coast and inland to form the Namib Desert. A thorough, thorough washing over many millions of years and yet the feldspar (clay) content remains unrealistically high and the quartz yield very low. This is not so much implausible as downright impossible!

A problem further compounded by the fact that this is supposed to be reworked sand. "Reworked" means the sand has undergone at least one previous phase of weathering, erosion and deposition. What we should be seeing here is something analogous to the aforementioned virtually pure quartz deserts (90 per cent) such as the Sahara or Arabian deserts. After all, the standard model dictates they gained high quartz content as a direct result of fluvial action.

The reader will also notice a distinct lack of shell material recorded in the samples, why is this? The Namib sand stretches for many hundreds of miles along the coast – in a process taking many millions of years it was washed by ocean waves and blown inland by the wind. Consequently, there should be an abundance of broken bits of shells mixed with the sand. Shells are much weaker than quartz so perhaps they were swiftly broken and ground down (in solution?) by the harder minerals. This may be possible under certain circumstances but not here because if the shells were subjected to a vigorous pounding and washing then how do we explain the high feldspar content? Were they not subjected to the same processes? Wouldn't the clay-forming feldspars have all but disappeared? You can't have it both ways.

As with most sand accumulations, the Namib Desert presents us with many oddities (some of which we haven't covered) and ultimately another vast ocean of sand of unknown origin – believed to have originated from mainly recycled material, there isn't even a hint as to the whereabouts of a granitic source. With this in mind, how can any method of dating be relied upon?

Nubian Sandstone revisited

We turn our attention back to the largest deposit of lithified quartz sand on the planet, the Nubian Sandstone, which, in underlying two of the largest dune formations on Earth – the Sahara and Arabian deserts – is also thought to be their source.

As mentioned earlier, the volume of the Nubian Sandstone works out to approximately 8 million cubic kilometres and in order to produce this, a staggering forty million cubic kilometres of granite intrusions would have to be weathered and eroded away. It is calculated such quantities would reach a height of approximately 267 metres on the continents – and this doesn't even include the overlying sand of the Arabian and Saharan deserts! Indeed, in total, we'd be closer to 300 metres in height. Even if some believe the figures quoted are an overestimation (if anything I would suggest the opposite) and we halve them, we are still looking at unfathomable volumes.

With such impressive volumes of sand you'd be forgiven for thinking that tracking down its respective granitic source would be a relatively easy task. Unfortunately, this is not the case.

> "The manner of formation of the famous Nubian sand-stone has been a matter for controversy for a century. This may be partly attributed to its wide geographical distribution (extending over 30° of longitude and 20° of latitude)1, its great vertical range (ranging from Palæozoic to Mesozoic), lack of fossils in its greater part, monotony of its lithological characters, and the difficulties entailed in the investigation of almost inaccessible localities in which it outcrops."
> Geology of the Nubian Sandstone. N. Shukri.
> Nature 156, 116-116 (28 July 1945)

More recent studies suggest that Nubian Sandstone owes its primary origin to tectonic activity and numerous subsequent recycling events.

> "Thus, the most probable provenance of the Lower Cretaceous (Nubian) sandstone is the recycling of relatively proximal Palaeozoic sandstone. Since first unroofed from above pan-African terranes closer to the secession of orogeny, the ensuing siliciclastics were recycled repeatedly throughout the Phanerozoic with little additional basement denudation. The Lower Cretaceous (Nubian) sandstone comprises

quartz sand that was first eroded from above pan-African orogens ca 400 Myr prior to deposition." [Author's parentheses]
(Origin of Lower Cretaceous ('Nubian') sandstones of North-east Africa and Arabia from detrital zircon U-Pb SHRIMP dating. Sedimentology, Kolodner et al., 2009)

In short, it would seem the sand is a gazillion years old and was created during and around the time of the Pan-African orogeny, which was a series of major Neoproterozoic orogenic events (mountain building) related to the formation of the supercontinents Gondwana and Pannotia, about 600 million years ago. After its birth the sand underwent a series of recycling events.

As I'm sure you will agree it's all very vague and there seems to be little concept of the amount of granitic intrusions required to create so much sand. To repeat, granite comes to the surface only in limited areas. It forms below Earth's surface and becomes exposed only after overlying sedimentary material has eroded away – a process that can take many tens of millions of years. With this in mind, and taking into account the quantities of sand involved, the regions in question should be littered with many hundreds of thousands granitic "prunes" – is this the case? Not even close!

Granitic outcrops (and boulders) occur *sporadically* in the Atlas Mountains, the central Hoggar (Ahaggar) Mountains, the Tibesti Mountains and the Air Mountains (central north part of Niger). They are, however, most frequent in the Red Sea Hills, or Mountains (Eastern Desert), which flank both sides of the Red Sea. Here an impressive array of granitic domes big and small spectacularly protrude the landscape, none more so than at Aswan on the Nile River (Aswan granite batholith). An area extensively mined for its granite and granodiorite by the Ancient Egyptians.

Despite the above, if we were to take a look at the broader picture here and collectively add all the granite intrusions together (regardless of variety and age [some are believed to be younger than others]) they would probably only amount to about 1 per cent of the land area in question (Sahara, Arabia, etc.). It is thus inconceivable for such an insignificant quantity of outcrops to have ever contained enough source rock (40 million cubic kilometres) to create in excess of 8 million cubic kilometres of sand – absolutely impossible! So where are the missing plutons?

Conventional wisdom would no doubt suggest several phases of continental uplift and erosion over billions of years has all but dissipated the evidence. This is not possible for the following reasons. The plutons seen today are largely dated to Precambrian or Cambrian times – in other words, they have been around for 500 to 600 million years. The timescale deems they obviously played a part in the production of the Nubian sand, especially those in the region of the Eastern desert mountains (Red Sea Hills). Unless geologists are prepared to rewrite Earth's history on this, there can be no doubt. What this means is North Africa, Arabia and even parts of Asia Minor should still be littered with the eroded remnants of infinite numbers of granitic plutons. When taking into account the hard and tough nature of granite, the evidence here should be unequivocal whereas this is clearly not the case. As a side thought, I would actually doubt whether all the granite outcrops in the world were ever large enough to supply the Nubian Sandstone.

Let us for a moment imagine that there was once enough source rock to create the "Nubia". Can you imagine the volume of water required to decouple the quartz grains from several million cubic kilometres of granite rock. How long did this take? Did it rain incessantly in the same region for billions of years? Very doubtful, eternity plus one wouldn't be enough time. Some may postulate the possibility of weathering in a subaqueous environment. Again, not possible, for that would take even longer and result in a more unconsolidated mix of sand, silt and clay – there'd be little in the way of the virtually pure quartz deposits seen today.

The time periods mentioned above cover lengthy epochs of major tectonic activity (the opening of the South Atlantic, the formation and breakup of the supercontinent Gondwana, etc.) and ensuing extensive magmatism, uplift, earthquakes, floods (and the rest), and yet we are expected to believe that the Nubian sand not only managed to remain pure but was also deposited in one basic location over and over again – this sounds highly improbable.

THE ROCK CYCLE

The concept of the rock cycle is attributed to James Hutton (1726–97), the 18th-century founder of modern geology. The main idea is that rocks are continually changing from one type to another and back again, as forces inside the earth bring them closer to the surface (where they are weathered, eroded, and compacted) and forces on the earth sink them back down (where they are heated, pressed, and melted). https://tatiana-sciencecorner.wikispaces.com/Rock+Cycle

The Rock Cycle

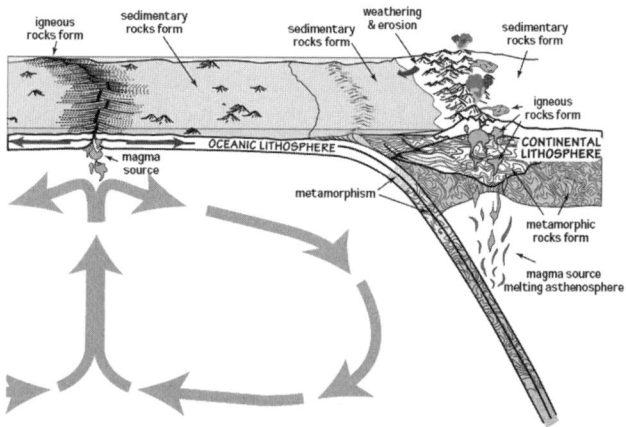

Source: http://commons.wikimedia.org/wiki/File:Rock_cycle_nps. PNG

So the elements that make up rocks are constantly being recycled, or so it is believed.

In short, it goes something like this: Uplift of igneous rocks => weathering => erosion and transport => deposition => burial and lithification => deformation and metamorphism => melting => solidification => and round and round.

Rock Cycle called into Question

Is there anybody brave enough to challenge this heretofore seemingly impregnable bastion of geological principles? This author will, via a simple question: how does granite form if all the feldspars dissolve in solution down rivers, streams, etc.? Let me put it another way: how can such enormous deposits of virtually pure quartz sandstone (e.g. Nubian, Navajo, Coconino, etc.) go through the rock cycle to re-emerge as granite with a diminished quartz content of only 20 per cent? What happened to all the quartz? Where did all the feldspars appear from? How on earth do we get back to granite consisting of 80 per cent feldspar and 20 per cent quartz? What process manages to effectively swap the quartz grains for the feldspars?

It makes little sense, no matter how you look at it – what we should be seeing here is virtually pure sandstone moving through the rock cycle to emerge at Earth's surface (upthrusted volcanic intrusions or otherwise) comprising of roughly the same pure quartz content as it did prior to subduction. This is clearly not the case – igneous rocks consisting of almost pure quartz grains *do not* exist (if they did, they wouldn't be called granite!). Considering the volumes of quartzite sandstone (and dunes) covering the Earth, how can this be?

Unless geoscientists come up with a feasible process whereby the feldspars are reintroduced there is obviously a big problem here, not only with granite, but by extension the rock cycle as well – it clearly doesn't work. What's more, if there is no rock cycle, it logically follows there must be a problem with the whole theory of plate tectonics (continental drift, subduction, uplift, etc.). Often purported as fact, when only a theory, it is suggested here that plate tectonics are one of Earth scientists' biggest faux pas that will one day soon come tumbling down! This author supports the "expanding Earth" or "growing Earth" hypothesis, which asserts that the position and relative movement of continents is largely due to the volume of Earth increasing. The biggest obstacle facing "growing Earth" proponents has always been: where did the additional mass come from? As we progress it will become apparent that Earth gained additional mass due to "recent" planetary chaos and the subsequent "accretion" of extraterrestrial volatiles, dust and debris.

Summary

Consensus is not a substitute for evidence and has no bearing on the truth.

The primary purpose of the last few chapters has been to call into question the consensus view as to the origin of sand. Although we've discussed some of the largest accumulations in the world, we haven't had to scratch too far below the surface to discover there is something drastically awry here. Provenance studies are tenuous at best – they are based on the uniformitarian assumption of a slow and gradual change over gazillions of years – there's hardly a hint of catastrophism and the possibility of rapid deposition of sedimentary material. But above all, what the evidence is clearly telling us is there was never enough source rock to create so much sand – consequently granite CANNOT be the source of world's quartz sand, it is downright impossible! But if sand didn't originate from granite, then from where?

A Smoking Gun

What follows is a rough chronological order for how the current configuration and characteristics of the solar system came into being. It is necessary to look at this as it will ultimately provide us with the primary source for the majority of Earth's sands (and tons of other stuff!).

Approximately 6,000 to 7,000 years ago (before that, who knows), the solar system differed considerably from today. Embracing the expanding earth theory; Earth was ~40 per cent smaller and all of today's continents were joined together as a single planetary landmass. There may have been shallow seas, small streams and lakes (and a few roaming dinosaurs) but the oceans we see today did not exist! This immediately goes a long way to resolving the problems of how prehistoric cultures such as the Clovis people managed to migrate across continents divided by vast oceans – they didn't, they simply walked across the land. Other enigmas also fall into place if we adopt the once "smaller Earth" theory.

The planets Venus and Mercury did not exist and "small Earth" had no Moon. Mars was a lush green planet replete with landmasses, oceans and an atmosphere. It was a replica of Earth as it stands today only slightly smaller. Mars harboured abundant life – *including humans* the same as you and I (but that's another story). It orbited much where it does today.

Around 6,000 years ago (4,000 BC) cosmic chaos began when a giant interloper entered our solar system and smashed into the *solid* planet Jupiter. It caused an apocalyptic explosion, which resulted in the birth of Venus and unimaginable quantities of space debris which engulfed the solar system. Among the debris was a small body that would eventually become our Moon.

On the outer planets: as first proposed by physicist catastrophist J. Ackerman there is no such thing as "gas giants". Jupiter and Saturn are *solid* planets as too are the other Jovian planets. They appear as gaseous bodies because they are still in turmoil as a result of recent cosmic chaos and the birth of Venus. Essentially they are still settling down as are the other planets in the solar system, including that of Earth.

The evidence for Venus' genesis remains today in the form of Jupiter's Great Red Spot (erroneously believed to be a raging storm) and the Asteroid belt that is a rocky band of debris located roughly between the orbits of Mars and Jupiter. Jupiter's GRS is still shrinking as things continue to settle out.

Note: I'm also open to the idea that interactions between Saturn (Sokar) and Jupiter (Ptah) may have resulted in the birth of Venus from Jupiter. Either way we have a scolding hot (hot enough to melt lead) new planet in the form of

Venus and a large corresponding birthmark (over three times the size of earth) on the face of Jupiter.

The initial "big bang" caused a shock wave which reverberated around the solar system wreaking havoc, including knocking the planet Uranus on its side and instigating close encounters between Jupiter and Saturn (forming Saturn's rings) which continued well into historical times.

There were probably a number of similar 'shock wave' events or eruptions as Jupiter continued to churn out tons of dust and debris for millennia. On Earth I would tentatively link some of these to mass extinction events such as the Cretaceous-Tertiary boundary (K-T) event associated with demise of the dinosaurs, and the Younger Dryas boundary event (YDB), which resulted in tons of material raining down on Earth. The former (K-T), I would link to the big bang Jupiter–Venus episode, the latter (YBD) perhaps to a time when the newly born Comet Venus rampaged through the solar system and disturbed Mars with a catastrophic glancing blow in the process. However, the conventional dates of 65 million and 12,900 years ago, respectively, should be dismissed out of hand. They are largely based on the false assumption that sedimentary layers are laid down over millions of years. This is incorrect; dust and debris from space is the source of large amounts of Earth's sedimentary deposits and these were laid down very rapidly, sometimes within a matter of days. The eruption of Mount St. Helens in Washington State, U.S. on May 18, 1980 teaches us that the stratified layers commonly characterizing geological formations can form very rapidly by flow processes. I would move the K-T and YDB events to around 6,000 to 7,000 years ago with consideration towards only a thousand years or less separating them – millions of years do not even enter the equation.

Tons of debris rained down on Earth following the birth of Venus – this additional mass caused Earth to slowly grow in size forcing the continents apart. But this isn't even half the story. Following a global "dark age" (YDB?) of approximately 5,200 years ago (3,200 BC) civilisations around the world began to emerge, such as the Egyptian, Sumerian, Indus civilisations, etc. (This was largely due to pockets of people managing somehow to migrate from Mars to Earth). Venus (with the moon in tow) disturbs Mars (glancing blow) from its orbit and they both take on highly erratic orbits in the vicinity of Earth's orbit. This leads to hundreds of encounters with Earth – a "celestial dance" that lasts over 3,000 years. From the perspective of ancient cultures it became a perennial cycle of death and rebirth as Mars and Venus appeared to move back and forth to Earth.

After approximately 2,000 years of encounters with Earth, the huge gravitational and electromagnetic forces exerted upon Mars caused a momentous event. The larger "magnet" of Earth literally tore out the smaller magnetic heart of Mars. Its solid iron core, its working dynamo, was sucked out to become the planet known as Mercury (Egyptian Aten). A "Glorious Sun-Disc of all Lands" is born! The evidence for the genesis of Mercury is still visible today in the form of the Valles Marineris – an enormous scar on the surface of Mars with a length approximately the same diameter as Mercury – this is no coincidence!

The Valles Marineris "birthmark" dominates the Martian landscape. It stretches over 4,000 kilometres (2,500 miles) across Mars, mostly east–west just below the equator. This enormous fissure is the legacy of when the solid iron core of Mars was sucked out to become the "winged messenger" – the planet Mercury.

Source: NASA.

I would like to point out that it was catastrophist J. Ackerman who first proposed Mercury was birthed from Mars, only he proposes it re-entered Mars several times over. I would suggest this "second sun" event occurred just once as recorded in the Egyptian Amarna Period which records the emergence of a new sun god called the Aten (Mercury).

After its birth, Mercury joined Mars and Venus in their celestial encounters with Earth. They were granted the status of divine god-kings and queens as they approached Earth, only to "die" as they moved away to become gigantic stars in the Kingdom of Osiris (the firmament of heaven). Amidst this cosmic melee, the Moon, assisted by Mars and Venus was slowly pulled into orbit around the Earth. Its erratic orbit settled into its recognisable 28½ day monthly cycle in a process that took several hundred years.

The birth of Mercury signalled the beginning of the end of cosmic chaos. It was as though a cosmic elastic band snapped allowing the planets to move away from the Earth to settle into relatively stable orbits around the Sun. Mercury and Venus became the first and second rocks from the Sun, while Earth was third and Mars was fourth, leaving the Moon to become Earth's permanent companion.

Cosmic chaos fallout

It is difficult to conceive of the amount of debris created as a result of the events of above. Venus was a planetary fireball – a flaming body of molten rock billowing out trillions of tons of dust and gases. Combined with the solar wind this gave Venus the appearance of a "plumed comet" exactly as recorded in the headgear worn by the divine queens of ancient Egypt.

Comet Venus. The headgear worn by the divine queens of ancient Egypt are a direct representation of Venus as it appeared in ancient times. Note the squashed oval shape of the disk. We will discuss this later.

Credit: Hedwig Storch Wikimedia Commons

Even though Comet Venus scattered tons of material throughout the solar system this was mainly of a gaseous composition – there was little in the way of rocky debris. Essentially, Comet Venus was a new planet in the process of cooling down – something it is still doing!

This would be in stark contrast to the dust, gases and rocky debris ejected from Mars. Mars really has to be singled out. Mars was once an Earth-like planet in every sense. It was home to a magnetic field, an atmosphere, large oceans and was once teeming with life (our ancestors). Over a period of about 3,000 years (Pharaonic Egypt), all this was obliterated as Mars was systematically torn apart upon close approach to Earth.

It convulsed internally and externally on an unimaginable scale – this manifested in a number of ways. Its surface became a seething cauldron of bubbling, boiling hot lava lakes and "snaking" lava rivers as thousands of fire-spitting super volcanoes (which played a part in origin of the Egyptian cobra) and fissures erupted across the Martian globe. Its protective magnetic shield was torn down as its solid iron core (its dynamo, Mercury) exited through the Valles Marineris. On-going encounters also saw tons of material stripped from the northern hemisphere of Mars. Erroneously believed to have been caused by a mega impact (Wiki), this now forms the North Polar Basin, which falls to a depth of 6 kilometres and covers a whopping 40 per cent of the planet. In addition to this, oceans boiled and countless tons of volatiles, vaporised rock and iron, dust and debris were either blasted out into space or stripped from the Martian surface by the solar wind.

Dead Parrot

To gain some kind of idea of the apocalyptic events to have befallen Mars (home) I have suggested in previous works that it would be like placing Earth in some kind of erratic cosmic washer-dryer for 3,000 years with the setting on melt! It has been tossed, shaken, stirred, boiled and set alight, all of which has transformed it from an Earth-like planet to a now virtually dry, barren, frozen world. Essentially, Venus cooled down while in contrast Mars has battled itself to death. As a "battling" incandescent red orb that loomed larger than the Sun, it is no wonder Mars was named after the Roman God of War. Warring Mars is now quite literally a "shell" of its former self – it is an ex Earth-like planet. All of which means Mars has lost a colossal amount of debris (mass). What happened to this?

Mars' loss is Earth's gain

As you would expect, large amounts of debris fell back to the Martian surface littering the landscape with rocks, boulders and vast expanses of sand and dust; not too dissimilar to what we see today. However, post-apocalyptic events also no doubt played a part in shaping modern-day Mars (cooling down for a start). But none of this even begins to compare to the colossal amounts of debris that fell to Earth. As with Mars, this would also include large rocks, boulders, stones, lots of water and sand. All this and more was swallowed up by Earth and to a large part is responsible for the majority of the sedimentary deposits laid down across the globe, especially on the continental blocks. Here we have material believed to be indigenous to Earth whereas it is actually from Mars.

This would also include Earth's oceans – indeed, Earth's water owes its existence to the depletion of the oceans that once covered parts of the red planet. In support of this I would ask, where do scientists think the oceans on Mars disappeared to? The answer is a simple one: they were sucked up by Earth during the many Earth/Mars encounters in the not-too-distant past. There was no great flood though, no one-off biblical event. Earth's accumulation of water and other material occurred over a period of about three or four millennia. Furthermore, Martian water (along with dust and debris) is still falling to Earth in the shape of noctilucent (night-shining) clouds, which form in Earth's upper atmosphere (mesosphere) and consist of tiny ice crystals with nuclei of meteoric "smoke".

Proponents of the expanding Earth hypothesis have always struggled to explain how Earth gains extra mass. The accretion of material from Mars more than answers this, especially when considering Mars has had its top blown off. Mass is from outer space, it is extraterrestrial. The last 7,000 years plus has seen an increase in Earth's mass, gravity, surface area and diameter due to the accumulation of massive amounts of material (mass) from Mars. Essentially, Earth has expanded by about 30 to 40 per cent in an extraordinarily short period of time. It is still expanding as it continues to vacuum up the remnants of recent chaos on a daily basis – only now this is on such a small scale it is virtually undetectable (prediction: Earth will be one day shown to be expanding).

The process of planetary differentiation (the denser materials of a planet sink to the centre while less dense materials rise to the surface) has caused Earth to expand or bulge out from within. This in turn has pushed the continents apart via cracks in the ocean floor (as well as on land). These are the plate boundaries normally associated with plate tectonics and continental drift – the Mid-Atlantic Ridge (the longest mountain range in the world) would be a prime example. Since the whole theory of plate tectonics is in serious error, a more befitting description of these "constructive" cracks would be expansion joints.

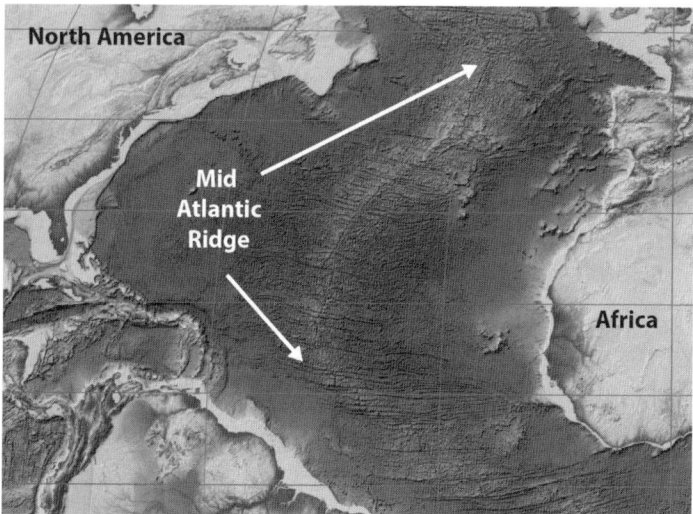

Mid-Atlantic "expansion joint".
Source: Author

As Earth expanded and the oceans began to fill and take shape the combined electromagnetic and gravitational effects (tidal forces) of close proximity bodies was dramatic. Mountains were suddenly dragged up; in some areas this would involve the raising of seafloors. Hence, fossilized seashells are found high in many mountains, the Himalayas are a good example. In addition to this, valleys were torn out, rivers and lakes formed, volcanoes erupted, earthquakes shook the world, incessant electrical discharges in the form of sprites and jets lit up the heavens, auroral manifestations danced across the sky day and night, and mass extinctions unfolded. Basically, everything you'd expect to happen if Earth was involved in encounters with other planetary bodies happened. And much of this is recorded in the geological record.

But as mentioned earlier, such events did not take place over billions, millions or even tens of thousands of years, not even close; multiple cataclysmic events began around 7,000 years ago and lasted at least 5,000 years, and at least 3,000 of these years spanned historical times. (I would also add something else occurred in the heavens in the first millennium AD). As a consequence, the current surface of Earth is of recent formation and very young. Indeed, the geology of Earth should be condensed into just a few millennia. This of course flies in the face of dating methods, and I would strongly argue, rightly so. It is simply not the case that we have reliable and accurate absolute dating methods. Radiocarbon dating and other radiometric dating techniques give an illusion of mathematical precision, which is unjustified.

The assumption of constant rates of decay under any condition (for radiometric dating) and the assumption of reasonably constant carbon levels (for C14 dating) in the past would not be applicable under the dynamic and catastrophic conditions as described above. The very fact that C14 has to be "calibrated" is an indication that something isn't quite right. This may be circular reasoning on my part but a simple web search for 'problems with carbon dating' will highlight the many issues with dating. I would suggest relative dating as the only dating method worthy of consideration.

This author is under no illusion of the daunting, if not insurmountable task to prove any of the above. Be that as it may, the quest has begun. To date, most of my work has been concentrated on the first civilisations (around 3,000 BC) and how and where it is written down errant planets danced with Earth during historical times – the Ancient Egyptians being my main field of expertise. With their myriad of cosmogonical deities and divine Horus kings, they have virtually laid the whole thing out for us – the Pharaonic Period is a time-ordered account of planetary catastrophe and virtually every aspect of Egyptian life was dictated by events in the heavens. I will provide a few examples of this towards the end of the book, but for now, we return to a new direction for the GKS: how the geological evidence is also staring us in the face.

EXTRATERRESTRIAL SANDS (ETS) –
A RADICAL NEW PARADIGM

During the many encounters with Earth a seething hot molten Mars not only ejects volatiles, dust and debris, it also churns out immeasurable quantities of vaporised rock, or rock vapour. Masses of which are also captured by Earth. It was probably a two-stage event which saw clouds of vapour initially re-condense in the coldness of space, forming vast interstellar clouds of sand-sized glass beads or droplets (amorphous). These fell to Earth and being so small instantly burned up (vaporised) for a second time. Earth's atmosphere subsequently becomes heavily laden with rock vapour, water, clay minerals, dust and debris (assisting in hazing the sun red). The rock vapour becomes so concentrated that silica based nanoparticles begin to precipitate (condense) out of the atmosphere. These rapidly grow as they fall to earth, crystallising in the process to form quartz and feldspar grains. Or, to put it another way – it rained sand!

A brief analogy would be rain and how water vapour in the atmosphere condenses into water and falls as raindrops. I am proposing a similar phenomenon occurred with rock vapour – huge quantities condensed into grains of sand and fell to Earth. The grains' size, shape and colour would be determined by such things as varying condensation rates, moisture content, density of elements and temperature. All this and the many variables that go with it played a part in shaping the sand from heaven.

Sand is Extraterrestrial!

Immeasurable volumes of sand fell to Earth to form virtually all the world's sand deposits. This would include all the aforementioned sandstone accumulations (Nubian, Coconino and Navajo) as well as the sandy deserts (Saharan, Arabian) and beaches of the world. All this and more originated from outer space. Indeed, quartz sand is anywhere and everywhere imaginable on Earth (even Antarctica) because it rained down from the sky. The so-called gazillion year "rock cycle" plays little part in the production of sand. Furthermore, there were no Milankovitch cycles, no glacial and interglacial periods, just many episodes of planetary catastrophe and the subsequent accretion of sand and debris. Before we delve into this in a little more detail let us briefly adopt the celestial sand notion and see how many things immediately begin to "fall into place", quite literally! A case in point would be the largest deposit of lithified quartz sand on the planet, the Nubian Sandstone. There is now no need to even attempt to source the impossible volumes of granitic rock required to create so much sand since granite outcrops were never the source – the sand fell from above and judging by the volumes and areas covered, this was one hell of an event.

Similarly, we recall the Navajo Sandstone in the western U.S., which supposedly originated from the Appalachian granite "prunes" far to the east before being transported via an immense transcontinental river system to the west. A process that apparently took many millions of years and involved the transportation of 100,000 cubic kilometres of sand some 1,250 miles (2,012 kilometres) across North America. As demonstrated, there was never enough granite to produce the unquantifiable volumes of sand involved here. More than that, there is absolutely no evidence whatsoever for a transcontinental river system – the whole thing is absurd and now we know why. The Navajo Sandstone, like so many other formations, is extraterrestrial in origin. It was laid down in yet another phase of cosmic chaos whereby many tons of rock vapour re-condensed and fell to Earth forming a fantastic sand pile.

The Navajo, and the Coconino for that matter, were originally desert-created sandstones, i.e. sand dunes (similar to the Sahara) that became lithified (turned to stone). From an extraterrestrial (ET) perspective, this tells us they were laid down pretty much where they lie today – a process that probably took just a few tens of years, certainly not millions of years. Both deposits were subsequently buried by other sediments and now make up just one of the many layers of sedimentary rock laid down in and around the Colorado Plateau (including the Grand Canyon).

The Plateau is made up of many layers of limestone, sandstone, siltstone and shale (mixed with occasional igneous intrusions and lava flows). Is all this stuff extraterrestrial, i.e. from Mars? I would say the majority of it is. It is reasoned that the aeolian sand layers (of which there are many) were largely ET. So, in one way or another, the other layers are also highly likely to have originated from Mars. This would include the skeletal fragments of marine organisms that make up most of the limestones – again, all from Mars.

Unlike the sand, the sedimentary material more associated with water such as limestones, probably didn't fall where they lie today. On the contrary, there is absolutely no doubt post-depositional geologic processes such as torrential rain, floods, tsunamis, high winds, volcanic eruptions, earthquakes and land upthrust (due to close proximity bodies), etc., etc., all played (and continue to play) a big part in shaping any "fallout" from Mars (and other bodies). The Grand Canyon is a prime example – many of the strata here were laid down in fairly rapid succession or even simultaneously as a result of floodwaters or shallow seas. This is why many sedimentary layers of the Grand Canyon run horizontally (lay flat) – they are fluvial deposits. The Navajo and Coconino Sandstones, on the other hand, formed as sand rained down during dryer times. Some layers would of course be mixed, containing both alluvial and aeolian (ET) material.

The Colorado Plateau uplifts and cracks open (EE) possibly the same time as a tsunami, hence the Grand Canyon is born. Having strata laid down rapidly would go a long way to explaining the unconformities (apparent gaps of some millions of years in the rock strata) that exist not just in the Grand Canyon but also throughout the world. There are no missing strata! Materials were washed in here and there. The result is strata that starts, covers an area, and then stops. In some areas it got twisted and turned (turbidites?) when the sediment was still relatively soft and pliable. The situation worldwide is exactly as we would expect to find it bearing in mind the 'recent' catastrophic events described above. They say Earth's history is recorded in the rock strata, it certainly is – it is a definitive record of planetary catastrophe lasting about 6,000 to 7,000 years.

Turning our attention to the sandy deserts of the world, in particular the aforementioned Sahara and Arabian deserts. It is now possible to understand how they were formed and any provenance issues simply disappear. Sand fell to Earth along the 30th parallel (emanating from the trans-Himalaya region) and quite literally "choked" lands that as the evidence clearly reveals were up until very recently sub-tropical paradises teeming with life. There's no need to disguise provenance in multiple recycling events or search out the nearest mountain range to pin your hopes on. No gazillion of years of erosion of an unknown source – no blasé consensus assumptions – no grey areas whatsoever. Sand rained down from above in great quantities in one of many episodic events lasting only a few hundred years. The fact that there remain large areas of unconsolidated sand (dunes) is testament to more recent deposits. The sudden and dramatic transformation of North Africa forced the human population to migrate to the Nile Valley where god-king planets and cosmogonical gods dictated whether or not they lived or died.

And then there are the world's quartz-rich beaches. Incalculable volumes of stones, pebbles and sand fell to

Earth, some on land, and some into the slowly expanding oceans (expanding earth). Wave action collected these and deposited them up along the coast to form our beaches. Some beaches are eroding at a rapid pace because they only formed recently. A good example here would be England's Jurassic Coast (south coast), which is said to have existed more or less where it is now for hundreds of thousands of years. And yet the mudstone cliffs are eroding at an alarming rate. How did they survive for so long when we can see with our own eyes how quickly they erode away?

It is not suggested for one moment that sand isn't being produced by the erosion of granite and deposited downstream on beaches. However, this is on such a minuscule scale as to be virtually negligible, totally ineffective as a source, let alone the problems of breaking up clusters of quartz grains. Rivers and streams producing quartz grains are from secondary sources, i.e. sedimentary material such as sandstones or lose sand merely washed off the land – the ultimate source of quartz sand has, and will always be extraterrestrial.

Recent accretion?

After all, what am I proposing here? Most scientists adhere to the theory that planets such as Earth formed via an accretion process whereby a disc of gas and dust settled into orbit about the host star – the bulk of accretion occurring within a few tens of millions of years. While I disagree with the whole solar nebular planetary formation theory (and the absurd dates) there is no doubt planets accrete mass. One look at the Moon, which has been pummelled by debris (from Mars), will confirm this. Now, what I am suggesting here is that during the last 6,000 to 7,000 years, Earth has accreted unfathomable quantities of dust and debris including that of sand. In other words, accretion has and does occur but it is most certainly not confined to a once basic event way back in "science fiction" times. It is an on-going dynamic process periodically boosted by chaotic events in the heavens, much of which involved the accumulation of sand. Indeed, Earth has undergone several sand accretion events in the last few thousand years. Some of the more recent deposits (such as the Sahara Desert) remain loose and unconsolidated (dune sand); other deposits have been subjected to post-geologic processes such as lithification as a result of burial (e.g. Nubian Sandstone). As mentioned earlier, most "sand events" are recorded in the rock strata; all of which leads to spurts of growth and an expanding Earth. It would seem we are going through a relatively stable period at the moment. That being said the "real history" of Earth deems this won't last.

EARTH'S METALLIC LAYERS – THE MESOPHERE

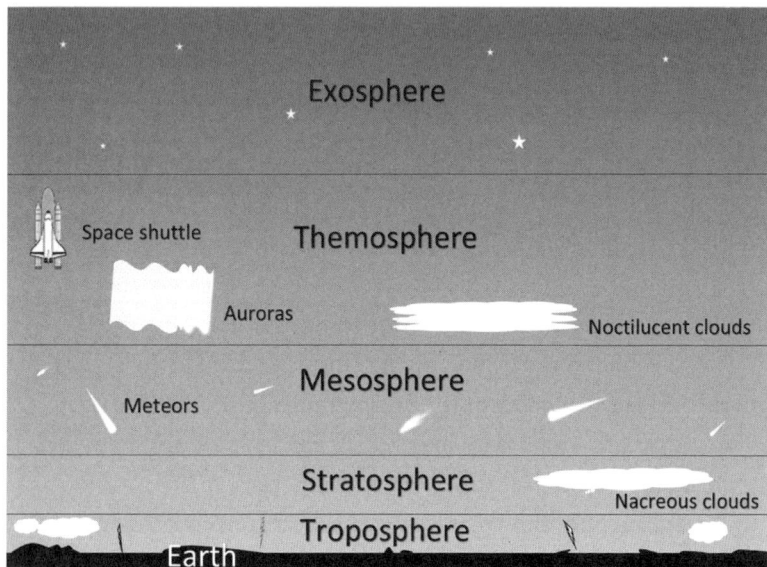

Diagram of the layers of Earth's atmosphere.
Source: Author.

Look up on a clear starry night and you'd be forgiven for believing not much exists between yourself and the stars – it appears to be void, just empty space. However, looks can be very deceiving. Even though we consider space to be empty, if all the material between the Sun and Jupiter were compressed together it would form a moon 25 kilometres across

(Universetoday.com). Earth's atmosphere is also littered with cosmic dust. In support of my thesis, we will now take a look at this in a little more detail. As we shall see, the vaporisation and precipitation of space material isn't such a farfetched idea as some may think. It is in fact an event that occurs above our heads on a daily basis. Furthermore, it involves the very same elements required to create quartz and feldspars.

The Earth's atmosphere is divided into five layers:

1. Troposphere: this is the first layer above the surface and contains half of the Earth's atmosphere. Weather occurs in this layer.
2. Stratosphere: many jet aircrafts fly here because it is very stable. It is home to the ozone layer which absorbs harmful rays from the Sun.
3. Mesosphere: meteors or rock fragments burn up in the mesosphere, which begins at about 50 kilometres and extends up to about 90 kilometres. Noctilucent clouds (NLCs) are located in the mesosphere.
4. Thermosphere: auroras occur in the thermosphere. It is also where the space shuttle orbits.
5. Exosphere: outermost region of Earth's atmosphere, where molecular densities are low and the probability of collisions between molecules is very small.

Of interest here is the mesosphere where almost all asteroids, meteors and dust burn up to form Earth's "atomic metal layers".

> More than 100 metric tons of meteoric debris enters the Earth's atmosphere per day [Love and Brownlee, 1993],

most of it in the form of small meteoroid particles with sizes smaller than 1 mm. These consist mainly of metals like sodium (Na), Iron (Fe), silicon (Si), potassium (K), magnesium (Mg), Calcium (Ca) and various oxides. As meteoroid particles enter the upper atmosphere with typical speeds of 10-20 km/s, collisions with mesospheric air molecules will heat them to temperatures high enough to vaporise them. The evaporated material forms the Atomic Metal Layers, observed mainly in the height range between 80 and 105 km.

http://www.athena-spu.gr/~upperatmosphere/index.php?title=Metallic_Layers

Actually, although 100 metric tons are given, the estimates of how much meteoric material enters the Earth's atmosphere vary from 5 to 400 tons/day. There are two reasons for this wide spread of estimates. The first is the problems involved in measuring this quantity and the second is that different measurement techniques are sensitive to different size ranges of incoming meteoroids. I would suggest that even the highest figure is an underestimation. (http://hal.archives-ouvertes.fr/docs/00/30/16/53/PDF/acpd-6-5357-2006.pdf)

As we can see the mesosphere is home to some of the basic ingredients required for sand. We have silicon, essential for making quartz (silicon and oxygen), calcium, sodium and potassium, the most common elements in feldspars.

Now this is where it gets interesting. After vaporisation the material re-condenses to form "smoke particles," which ultimately fall to Earth.

A large fraction of the meteoroides entering the Earth's atmosphere oblate in the mesosphere at altitudes above 75 km. The oblated material composed of elements as iron, magnesium and silicon re-condenses to form nanometer-sized particles termed meteoric smoke... (MSPs)

Meteoric smoke particles of a few nanometers size form from the re-condensation of the oblated silicon oxides and metallic vapor compounds in the mesosphere. Ablation and smoke particle formation from the low-volatility vapors occurs mostly at altitudes of 80–100 km. The average initial size of the smoke particles at these altitudes is very uncertain. Hunten et al. (1980) estimate a range of 0.4–20 nm diameter and choose a value of 2.6 nm as the nominal case for their model simulations. Once formed, the particles grow by coagulation and by condensation of further oblated vapors in the mesosphere. Recent calculations with a one-dimensional model describe the development of the meteoric smoke particles in the mesosphere including processes of formation, coagulation, condensation and gravitational settling (Gabrielli et al., 2004).

They (MSPs) are assumed to follow the general motion (advection) of the air, gradually coagulating and sedimenting downward. This motion can transport the smoke particles down to the lower atmosphere where they can be taken up by clouds and finally rain out of the atmosphere.

http://www.atmos-chem-phys.net/5/3053/2005/acp-5-3053-2005.pdf

Scientists know less about the mesosphere than about other layers of the atmosphere. This is because weather balloons and jet planes cannot fly high enough and the orbits of satellites are above the mesosphere. There aren't many ways to get scientific instruments to the mesosphere to take measurements there. Some measurements are obtained using sounding rockets which make short flights but don't go into orbit. Overall, there's a lot we don't know about the mesosphere because it is hard to measure and study. Despite all of this, laboratory experiments undertaken at the University of Leeds imply that a major building block of meteoric smoke particles (MSPs) is silicon dioxide (SiO_2):

> An important component of this part of the project was to develop the first model of silicon chemistry in the upper atmosphere. The kinetic studies on reactions of Si^+, SiO^+, Si and SiO showed that silicon, freshly oblated from meteoroids, is quickly converted to very stable silica molecules. Hence, SiO_2 is expected to be a major building block of MSPs, along with Fe and Mg oxides.
> http://www.chem.leeds.ac.uk/john-plane/laboratory/mesosphere/past-research/inspect-silicon.html

Let us remember, the primary constituent of desert, beach and sandstones is quartz sand – a form of silicon dioxide (SiO_2). And here we are presented with a process whereby particles of silicon dioxide are precipitating out of the atmosphere! Could these nanoparticles be precursors to quartz and feldspars grains? I believe this is indeed the case. There is, however, a significant size difference between a grain of sand and a smoke particle (2 to 0.05 mm in diameter versus 0.4 to 20 nm). In addition, quartz is a crystallised form of silicon dioxide. So, how do we get from SiO_2 flecks to crystalline grains of sand?

Close encounters with Mars sees Earth's metallic layers (mesosphere) supersaturated with silicon-rich vapour (silicon monoxide gas) and other oblated material. This re-condenses to initially form MSPs, just as we see today. However, the density is such that the nanoparticles rapidly grow in size and fall to Earth, crystallising in the process – a grain of sand is born! The composition, size and colour of each grain would be determined by the volume and composition of incoming meteoric material.

For this idea to carry merit the first thing we would expect to see is a link between fluctuations in volume and particle size with the input of meteoric material. It is with no surprise that this is exactly what we find.

This coagulation effect can also be seen in the size distribution in Fig. 5, where an increase in meteoric input results in greater amounts of large particles. http://hal.archives-ouvertes.fr/docs/00/30/16/53/PDF/acpd-6-5357-2006.pdf

121

Particles grow as they fall

Comparing the measured data to a simple model of the photoelectron currents, we tentatively conclude that we observed MSPs in the 0.5–3 nm size range with generally increasing particle size with decreasing altitude.

http://www.ann-geophys.net/30/1661/2012/angeo-30-1661-2012.pdf

But this is today, and the solar system today has settled down somewhat. What if we were to drastically scale things up and ask what would happen if a major cosmic event caused the daily influx of space material to increase from around 100 tons to many tens of thousands or even millions of tons plus? What effect would this have on Earth's metallic layers and the formation of MSPs? Logic dictates both the quantity and the size of MSPs would increase. The key here is *density* – a denser vapour will increase volume and yield progressively larger particles – that is scientific fact.

Crystallisation

Can minerals condense from vapour? Absolutely! As we have seen, silica (SiO_2) exists in many different forms that can be crystalline as well as non-crystalline (amorphous). Our grains of sand are crystalline, meaning the silicon and oxygen atoms are arranged in definite regular patterns throughout. The burning question is: can minerals form from gas? More specifically: can quartz grains grow in the atmosphere as I propose? On this,

I wrote to Dr Matthew Genge (personal email 27/03/2013) the Senior Lecturer in Earth and Planetary Science at Imperial College, London and basically asked if quartz crystals could condense from the silicon vapour in the atmosphere? Dr Genge thankfully replied thus: "Mineral phases are very unlikely to condense in the atmosphere due to vaporised meteoroids because the density of metals is just too low."

A predictable response as the material entering Earth's atmosphere today is, by comparison to my proposed sequence of events, virtually negligible. However, he also added: "But you are right, minerals can condense from gas if the density is sufficiently high."

This is a crucial point – it offers strong support for the whole ET sand thesis. We have confirmation that if the "density is sufficiently high" it is absolutely possible for crystallised sand particles to rain out of the sky. This is exactly what I contend – past episodes of chaos caused the atmosphere to become supersaturated, so dense with rock vapour that vast oceans of sand re-condensed and rained down on Earth. In short, silica nanoparticles *are* precursors to quartz grains and feldspars, and their size, volume and crystallisation is directly associated with density. The next few pages will be dedicated to supporting this revolutionary premise.

The growth and size of quartz grains

A grain of quartz sand is many crystalline silica particles compressed into a single grain (http://ccc-wis.com/page8/page8.

html). This tells us that as particles fall, they increase in size by coagulation and by condensation of further particles in the atmosphere. Again, the main factor here would be density – a more concentrated gas producing larger grains. I am reminded of snowflakes that are a form of ice crystallisation (each one slightly different). Under certain storm conditions when convection is in the air, snowflakes may go up and down several times within clouds. This gives the ice crystals the opportunity to grow very large. A similar process may have also played a part in both the size and crystallisation of quartz grains.

Sand, as we have seen, comes in a variety of sizes ranging from course to fine (2.0 down to 0.02 millimetres). Setting aside some highly variable factors, one can envisage the finer grains forming in a less saturated environment whereas larger grains would condense out of a much thicker vapour. An example of a fine grain formation would be the Saharan and Arabian sands. Comprising some of the finest silk-like sand in the world this is a very recent deposit, and as a result has been less subjected to post-depositional processes (apart from mainly wind). Thus, what we see today hasn't altered much since it rained out of the sky only a few millennia ago. From this we surmise the density of Earth's mesosphere was such that only the precipitation of fine quartz grains could take place. This would be in contrast to some of the underlying medium to coarse-grained Nubian Sandstone, which must have been created during "denser" times.

On a cautionary note, we cannot rule out the possibility that once a certain level of saturation is reached, other factors may have dictated grain size (variables such as the efficiency of coagulation, the state and circulation of the atmosphere, temperature, and moisture content, etc.). All no doubt played a part in formation – but they may equally have been the primary factor in determining size after a certain saturation point.

Studies show that MSPs today take about ten days to form. (http://cedarweb.hao.ucar.edu/workshop/tutorials/2007/ plane_07.pdf). When taking into account the density factor I would suggest we are looking at a similar time period for the formation of sand grains.

Low-temperature crystallisation

Different minerals crystallize at different temperatures, olivine for example, crystallises at high temperatures whereas quartz crystallises at low temperatures. The temperature in the mesosphere down to the troposphere (ground level) varies from between -90°C to about 18°C (room temperature). There is nothing here to preclude the growth of quartz crystals. Indeed, quartz has been crystallized directly from seawater at room temperature. (http://europepmc.org/abstract/MED/17738438/ reload=0;jsessionid=vN1tuRiQFxcAB51xsRep.2)

Need I remind the reader, although not a totally aqueous solution, I propose quartz grains condensed out of an atmosphere heavily laden with clay-rich moisture. The source of this water, Mars.

Shape characteristics

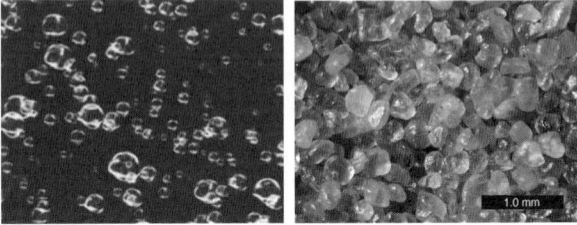

Left: raindrops. Right: quartz sand grains.
Source: Wikimedia Commons.

Contrary to popular belief raindrops are anything but the classic tear shape; they only have the "raindrop" shape when they're about to fall off something. Falling raindrops go through a complex cycle of splitting and joining as they fall. Larger raindrops become flattened at the bottom, like that of a hamburger bun, due to air resistance. The air resistance causes them to split into smaller raindrops. There is no single raindrop shape. However, very small raindrops (radius > 1 millimetre) are more spherical due to less surface area resistance. A good description of the larger drops would be along the lines of oblate ellipsoids.

It may be a tentative link but I believe it's possible to make a comparison between the shape of raindrops and our falling sand in that a cursory glance at the above images reveals they are not too dissimilar. Only on closer inspection do the more angular properties of sand become apparent. But this is to be expected; they are of a different composition. One's a fluid, precipitated

from water vapour in the air, the other is a tough crystal born
from rock vapour so it's prone to more jagged edges.

Roundness and Sphericity

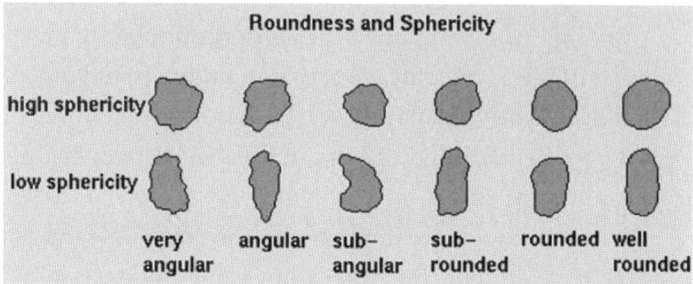

Roundness and Sphericity

high sphericity

low sphericity

| very angular | angular | sub-angular | sub-rounded | rounded | well rounded |

When quartz grains break away from granite they are
very angular, having angles or sharp corners. As they are
transported (initially by water) they become rounder as
their irregular edges are removed by abrasion. Beach sand
becomes highly rounded and bleached due to endless
rolling and bouncing in the surf… or so the consensus
thought pattern goes. Indeed, it is believed that the
roundness of grains is indicative of age, i.e. a more
rounded grain is indicative of erosion and rounding over
millions of years.

Everything seems to be in order here; it all seems to make sense
especially if the rock cycle were true and correct as most geologists
swear to. However, things aren't as clear cut as they seem. As
with the origin of quartz sand worldwide erroneous assumptions
abound. Time to throw another spanner in the works.

The concept that streams round their transported sands does not appear to be generally true; the available data indicate that stream sands usually remain angular or sands would be rounded if little or no coarse material were present and conditions of wear were gentle, but the writer does not know of a published description of such a case. The rounding of sand grains appears to occur chiefly in areas of sand concentration, that is, in dunes and on beaches. The evidence, however, is not sufficient to prove whether wind or wave actions most effective in rounding sand grains. Dune sands appear to show the best rounding, on the average, of any type of sediment, but this is not valid evidence in favor of the effectiveness of wind abrasion. Some data indicate that the roundness of dune sands is a property largely inherited from beach sands, the higher mean roundness of dune sands resulting from selective transportation of previously rounded grains. Regardless of which agent is most effective, experiments show that grains of sand size are rounded so slowly that well rounded grains probably have been subjected to more than one period of rounding.

Abstract: Effects of Transportation on sedimentary Particles, D Russell, Louisiana State University, Baton Rouge, Louisiana, May 25, 1938.

http://sp.sepmonline.org/content/sepsprec/1/SEC2.body.pdf

Further…

> Although one might wish to estimate quantitatively the distance of travel for sand from its average roundness or percentage of angular grains, this is as yet impossible because the processes of rounding are still poorly understood.
>
> (Pettijohn, 1987. Sand and Sandstone, p.79)

> To date, however, most studies of modern beach deposits do not show strikingly more rounded grains than their presumed continental source.
>
> (ibid, p.80)

> The nineteenth century wisdom was that aeolian sands were "perfectly rounded" like "millet-seed," and when real aeolian sands are examined, some are indeed found to be rounded. But many are poorly rounded.
>
> (Cooke, Warren, Goudie, 1993. Desert Geomorphology, p.314)

Another tenet of the so-called rock cycle called into question? Maybe, either way, sand doesn't seem to be performing as expected. After a gazillion years of transport by water most geologists assumed (many still do!) we would end up with "well-rounded" grains whereas the opposite seems to be true. If anything it is the action of wind on dune sands that appears to be responsible for rounding and not water. This is actually a fact that can be confirmed by taking a look at the biggest industry for sand – construction.

For the last 150 years sand mixed with concrete has shaped the contours of our increasingly urbanised world. Because of its low cost, strength and ease of use, this grey slurry has become the dominant building material around the globe. Dubai in the United Arab Emirates (UAE) provides an astonishing example of the appetite for sand. Within a few decades this once fishing village has morphed into a mecca of modern architecture.

Dubai's Palm Islands are perhaps one of the country's boldest megaprojects undertaken. Often referred to as the "eighth wonder of the world" the Palm Islands are artificial islands constructed from 5.5 million cubic metres of rock and 94 million cubic metres of sand which was dredged from the bottom of the Persian Gulf. Flying high in the seemingly endless supply of money and sand, in 2003 Dubai embarked on an even more extravagant project – "the world". This artificial archipelago consists of 300 islands designed as a map of the world. It required three times as much sand as the Palm Islands. The financial crisis of 2008 has all but brought a halt to construction but the crisis is more than financial – over development throughout the region has totally liquidated Dubai's' natural sand resources.

Like all the Gulf States, Dubai has sand everywhere, it is on the edge of the desert – they have all the sand they need. So, why doesn't the Emirate simply help itself to the desert? They would, but unfortunately it's the wrong kind of sand! Desert sands have been blown around by the wind and are typically very round and very smooth. Consequently, they are no good for building artificial islands because the grains don't stick together. If desert sands were used in concrete the slurry would slip and the concrete would have poor strength. More angular, rougher-edged sand is required – sand that naturally sticks together. Sea sand is perfect for island building and construction because it is more angular.

The growing demands of the construction industry and the lack of available marine sand means we now have a global shortage of the "right" sand. It's hard to believe but selling sand to the Arabs is now a reality. In some areas of the world this shortage has led to smuggling and the illegal mining of beach sand. (Source: "The Sand Wars" by Denis Delestrac http://sand-wars.com/synopsis.html)

What the above clearly reveals is that marine sand (sea, beach and river sand) is predominantly angular while dune sand is more rounded. A puzzling situation as sand is reputed to be tens of millions of years old (Let us also remember, the ocean floors are believed to be only 180 million years old). Shouldn't it all be well rounded by now? Essentially, what we have here is vast accumulations of sand of unknown provenance, some of which has undergone rounding by processes that are little understood. Only when taking into consideration the ET sand theory does any of this even begin to make sense.

Crystallising out of a moist atmosphere sand begins life naturally as very angular to sub-angular grains, their actual size dictated by the density of silica in the atmosphere. Small grains taking on a more spherical shape due to less surface area resistance – this being no different to the way small raindrops form. In one of many sand accretion events, enormous clouds of these angular grains fall to Earth. Some fall into the sea and wash up on the shores to form beaches, the rest falling on land, in places forming huge deposits of sand, i.e. the Sahara and Arabian deserts. Although some rounding may have taken place as grains collided during their descent, it is post depositional processes that are largely responsible for rounding.

Rounding is caused chiefly by wind action in areas of sand concentrations such as dune sand (mainly deserts). The wind causes the grains to collide and rounding to increase. Wave action also produces more rounded grains but to a far lesser extent. This is proven by the fact that marine sand (i.e. sea bed, beach and river) tends to be more angular than dune sand (as mentioned above). If it wasn't, then it wouldn't be such a sought-after commodity in the construction industry. Many beaches consist of angular quartz grains because they have only recently fallen to Earth, and thus less subjected to erosional processes. Rounding has and continues to take place depending on the intensity of wave action, i.e. lots of wave action will create more rounded and smoother grains of sand, whereas a more protected beach will have more angular sand. The same obviously applies to the action of wind on dune sand; exposure to stronger winds will result in rounder grains. The larger the grain the more rounding takes place, smaller grains remaining more angular. While there are many permutations to consider, may I suggest this basic framework be used when studying the rounding of grains.

Lyme Regis (UK) beach sand under a microscope.
Source: Author.

It is beyond the scope of this book to analyse each and every single sand deposit dotted around the globe. However, armed with the above, let us take a brief look at some of the previously discussed accumulations with a view to demonstrating just how much sense this makes.

As we know, Nubian Sandstone underlies a vast area of North Africa, Arabia, etc.

> Under the polarizing microscope, Nubia sandstones are composed entirely of white to pale grey,

monocrystalline, sub-rounded to subangular, and medium to fine-grained quartz, which are cemented by iron oxides and/or clay minerals.
(http://www.geologicacarpathica.com/GeolCarp_Vol54_No5_329_336.html)

The Nubia is said to be tens of millions of years old ("super mature") and the result of numerous recycling events (as most sandstone formations). If this is indeed the case then shouldn't the grains be well rounded by now? Recycling means repeated weathering, erosion and transportation in one way or another, so why aren't we witnessing highly polished grains? Just exactly how many recycling episodes do you need before quartz grains become well rounded? Shouldn't we be seeing something analogous to the well-rounded overlying dune sands of the Sahara and Arabian deserts?

Let us remember, using the zircon dating method it is thought the Lower Cretaceous (Nubian) sandstone comprises quartz sand that was first eroded from above pan-African orogens circa 400 million years prior to deposition. The lack of rounding further confirms there is something seriously wrong with such dating techniques. The dates do not correspond with the physical evidence.

The Nubia is not a gazillion years old; it is a recent ET formation. Its grains remain angular to sub-rounded because they were laid down in largely shallow marine environments (shallow seas; origin Mars?), where they lithified to form sandstone. Although some sand may have fallen in continental settings, the lack of rounding tells us wind has little part in shaping the sand (apart from perhaps during descent). In other words, the Nubia shows little sign of ever being dune sand.

Silica density determines grain size; we may compare this to the slow progression of a large band of rain crossing the US with some areas experiencing heavy rainfall and large raindrops, while other areas are subjected to persistent light rain and small raindrops. Certain areas may of course experience a combination of both within a few hours or days. There are an infinite number of permutations here as you would expect (it's called weather!). This would be a very similar situation to sand raining down from the heavens – with dense silica clouds producing larger grains than less dense clouds, which would precipitate finer grains. This would go a long way to explaining the variety of medium to fine-grained sandstone strata comprising the Nubian sandstone, indeed the sandstone variations throughout the world. Certain areas will have coarse-grained sandstones while other areas feature smaller-grained sandstones. And then there's everything in between with strata in some locations comprising of coarse-, medium- or fine-grained sandstone – on occasion, one layer on top of the other, in no particular order or pattern.

We may ask, if originating from the same granitic source, why aren't the Nubia quartz grains virtually all the same size and of the same roundness by now? Why the contrast, not only between certain layers but also regions? Whereas others may struggle to provide answers, the above is consistent with the ET sand model.

Nubian Sandstone also frequently includes strata of clay and shale and thin seams of coal or lignite. This tells us that as certain layers of sand began to harden, mud and silt washed over the land. This would be in the form of floodwater or tsunami-like conditions. Sedimentary layers that, as with the recent Mount St. Helens eruption, were laid down in a matter of days if not hours. Judging by the strata, there were multiple such events.

Now, turning our attention back Stateside to the Navajo and Coconino Sandstones. These were both once dune sands that turned to rock. Indeed, some have compared the Navajo Sandstone to once being very similar to the dunes of the Sahara today. The Navajo and Coconino like most aeolian sandstones, consist almost entirely of well-sorted, well-rounded quartz sand (http://www2.nature.nps.gov/geology/education/foos/zion.pdf). This bodes well with the ET sand theory only we have to dismiss the notion of an imaginary transcontinental river system transporting and depositing unfathomable quantities of sand over tens of millions of years. The sand fell from above and was subjected to wind action and this is what we see represented today.

There are dozens of similar aeolian sandstone formations throughout the world. Here is a list of some of the more well-known ones:

- The Tepeats Sandstone (Grand Canyon)
- De Chelly Sandstone (Arizona, Colorado, New Mexico, Utah)
- Casper formation (Wyoming)
- Aztec sandstone (Nevada)
- Rotliegendes (western and central Europe)
- Barun Goyot Formation (Gobi Desert basin)
- Cave Sandstone, Sambaiba formation (northern Brazil)
- Botucatu sandstone (Brazil and Uruguay)
- Frodsham member of the keuper formation (west and central Europe)
- Kinnerton Sandstone Formation (England)
- Lyons Sandstone (Colorado)
- Entrada Sandston (Wyoming, Colorado, northwest New Mexico, northeast Arizona and southeast Utah)
- Weber Sandstone (Utah and northwestern Colorado)
- Nugget sandstone (Utah, Colorado)
  (Sourced from Wiki)

The Gobi Desert. Is the sand the result of billions of years of erosion or are we looking at a more recent deposit.

Source: Wiki Commons

We pause briefly for a moment to once again ask the question central to this book, where did so much sand come from? Eroded and blown from where? Where's the parent rock?

As with the Coconino and Navajo all of the above display similar classic wind-blown features such as frosted sand grains and large crossbedding formed from dunes rather than currents because they rained down from the sky in a mostly dry environment.

We recall the Namib Desert, which flanks the Atlantic Ocean in southern Africa. The dunes here consist of sub-rounded to sub-angular grains (Brink, Engineering Geology of Southern Africa, Volume 4, Pretoria, 1985). Bewilderment would be an understatement! At over 55 million years old (one of the lower estimates) the Namib is reputed to be the oldest desert in the world. It is a coastal desert subjected to wind and wave action (consensus has it originating from the Orange River) and yet its grains are no more rounded than marine sand, how is that possible?

Flanked by the Atlantic Ocean enormous Namib Desert dunes.
Source: Robur.q Wikimedia commons.

It's possible because the Namib fell from the sky only recently, possibly only 2,000 to 3,000 years ago (could be less). It was largely dumped along the coast of southern Africa (some in the Atlantic Ocean) so recently that the process of rounding has barely begun. With the passage of time one would expect the grains to eventually show signs of becoming more rounded but this would depend entirely on the wind.

The Namib isn't the only dune sand to show a lack of rounding. On the contrary, it seems rounding is a rarity!

However, more recent studies have indicated that most quartz dune sand grains are not well rounded, the exceptions being cases where the sands have been recycled from older sedimentary units. (Author's Note: rounding as a result of reworking most certainly doesn't apply to the Nubian sandstones as they are sub-rounded to subangular!)

Goudie & Watson (1981) examined fine and very fine sand grains in 108 dune sand samples from different parts of the world and also found that <u>well rounded grains are relatively rare</u> (about 8% of the grains examined). In dune sands from the Thar and California the predominant shape was sub-angular, although the sands from other areas were found to be predominantly sub-rounded. Only samples from Tunisia showed a predominance of rounded grains. [Author's underlining]
Aeolian Sand and Sand Dunes, Pye & Tsoar. p.83 2009)

The author also cites the Simpson Desert, reputedly the world's largest sand dune desert covering an area of 176,500 square kilometres (68,100 square miles).

Most of the dune sand grains in the Simpson Desert of Australia are sub-angular to angular, with no noticeable rounding being accomplished in the present dune environment (Folk 1978). Folk suggested that this might be because the Simpson Desert dunes are partially fixed by vegetation and

140

the grains have not been blown great distances from
their fluvial source sediments.
(Ibid)

In summary and from a global perspective, the above offers overwhelming support for the ET sand theory. It is everything we would expect to see if dune sand is of recent origin. The majority of deposits worldwide are not well rounded as early geologists assumed, and modern-day geologists are baffled by, because they have fallen in regions where aeolian processes have yet to have a noticeable effect. The Simpson Desert is a prime example of a recent deposit that in places has barely moved, hence the mainly sub-angular grains. There are of course going to be a proportion of well-rounded grains where the sands have been blown about but as the studies above show, this is "relatively rare".

Big Red (Nappanerica) sand dune on the eastern edge of the Simpson Desert.

Source: Photo by Paul Hanly, 10 September 2007. Wikimedia Commons.

IN SEARCH OF LIFE –
WHERE ARE THE FOSSILS?

Fossiliferous means (of a rock or stratum) containing fossils or organic remains. Limestone that contains visible fossil remains is called fossiliferous limestone. These are normally shell and skeletal fossils of the organisms that produced the limestone. Unfossiliferous or non-fossiliferous means rock or stratum that contains no fossils. Most sandstones are surprisingly unfossiliferous – they contain little or no fossils. This would include the Navajo, Coconino and Nubian Sandstones.

You would be forgiven for thinking something isn't quite right here. The majority of sandstones are said to have been laid down over tens of millions of years and yet despite such incredible timescales, there is a clear and noticeable absence of fossils. How on Earth is this possible? Shouldn't the evidence for ancient life forms be in abundance? Where do geologists stand? Unfortunately, there isn't much on this – certainly little in the way of a plausible explanation as we shall see. It seems the environment just wasn't conducive to life or some kind of magical occurrence 'dissolved' away any organic (plants, animals) or inorganic material (shells).

> Sandstone does not usually contain good fossils because the energetic environments where sand beds form don't favour their preservation.
> http://geology.about.com/od/more_sedrocks/a/aboutsandstone.htm

Could this in anyway be correct? I strongly doubt it and if we take a look at how the Nubian Sandstone was supposed to have formed we can clearly see why.

> At possibly the largest sand deposit in the solar system we have seen how the Nubia spans an incredible four million square kilometers and ranges from 1,000 to 3,000 meters thick. Now here's the thing; consensus says it was deposited in a beach or nearshore shallow marine environment after being transported by the wind.
> (The Geology of Egypt, El Baz, 1984 p.576)

Indeed! Question: "…transported by the wind." From where?

I doubt I need to point out to the reader that *water means life* and a shallow marine environment means lots of it. The shallow seas that cover the continental shelves today are sunlit or neritic, waters where the oceans are most productive, where biomass is highest and where all the major sea fisheries of the world take their catches. In addition to fish we have sea urchins, sponges, clams, corals, algae and seagrasses to name just a fraction. The fact is the majority of all plant and animal life on earth is found in the oceanic ecosystems and the majority of these are in shallow marine environments. So why can't we find evidence of a similar but more primitive ecosystem recorded in Nubian Sandstone? Why does the Nubia, or any other sandstone for that matter, comprise essentially of pure quartz grains devoid of fossils?

The majority of the fossil record has been found after sediments in shallow water marine environments have become lithified – the Jurassic Coast of southern England is testament to this. The abundance of fossils here reflects the immense number of organisms that lived during this epoch. The laying down of the Nubia is said to span some 400 million years and incorporates many life-rich geologic epochs including that of the Jurassic Period (also known as the Age of Reptiles).

With this in mind, are we seriously expected to believe that at a time when dinosaurs roamed the land and sea levels were high and there was no polar ice, millions of square miles of shallow waters were devoid of life? Because this is what it amounts to if we are to accept the consensus view. Even allowing for periodic mass extinctions the lack of fossils makes no sense whatsoever.

If the Nubia was laid down in shallow seas then this is the type of environment where a plethora of organisms capable of forming calcium carbonate shells and skeletons would live. When these animals die their shells and skeletons usually get broken up into sand-sized pieces. Many beaches today contain tiny fragments of shell and coral mixed in with quartz crystals. Deep-water sediments also tend to be composed of the tiny skeletal debris from siliceous and calcareous skeletons of microscopic organisms. Nubian Sandstone is devoid of such remains – why? What of the weather, wind and tides? Are we to believe that no shell fragments were produced during the millions of years of sand deposition in shallow waters? Of course not. Marine life must have flourished under such conditions and the evidence should be unequivocal. If anything, what we should be seeing here is something analogous to the highly fossiliferous Jurassic mudstones and limestones that apparently formed in shallow waters along the south coast of England. Or, at the very least, evidence of shell and skeletal fragments (in the form of silicified microfossils) mixed in with the quartz grains. This is clearly not the case.

The main reason why geologists believe the Nubia was laid down in a shallow marine environment is because it contains beds of fossiliferous marine limestones and marls (clays and silt). These are deemed to have formed on the ocean floor in warm shallow seas (Nubian Sandstone, Wiki). Similar limestone beds are also found high in the Himalayas, also said to be once at the bottom of the ocean. While there is absolutely no doubt such layers were deposited in watery conditions something doesn't quite add up here, as we shall see.

Imagine for a moment a similar setting to that which created the Nubian limestone beds – a shallow marine environment teeming with life. The animals die, their shells sink to the seafloor and over millions of years (as per uniformitarianism consensus) a layer of limestone-forming material builds up.

Sounds plausible and it's difficult to argue against this, but then something inexplicable occurs. Sand begins to fall. Ton upon ton of unfossiliferous quartz-rich sand builds up on the layer of fossil-rich limestone, in some areas to a depth of several hundreds of metres. How is this possible? How can sand fall under the same marine (or freshwater) conditions and remain fossil-less? What possible process could explain the thick layers of virtually "sterile" sand intercalated with thin layers of abundant life? When considering how the sand is supposed to have been laid down over many millions of years we are presented with an impossible situation. But wait – it gets worse. After several millennia of fossil-free sands another bed of "life" appears. What brought about these sudden and dramatic changes?

Sandstones are mainly unfossiliferous because they consist of sand that fell from the sky. This would include the Nubian Sandstone, which was indeed transported by the wind! It formed as vast dense clouds of sand rained down over a relatively short period of time, probably a few years, if not less. There were many phases to the Nubian formation, which I tentatively link to the genesis of Venus from Jupiter around the time of the K-T event (?), roughly 6,000 to 7,000 years ago. A number of extremely thick layers were deposited in rapid succession under some very wet/moist conditions. This was not, however, an entirely shallow marine environment as is currently believed (see below). It was a moisture-soaked atmosphere where unfathomable volumes of quartz grains crystallised and fell to Earth encased in mineral-rich water droplets. The primary origin of this water was also extraterrestrial (possibly Jupiter, later definitely Mars). This being a phenomenon that continues even today in the form of noctilucent clouds (NLCs). Fluids/moisture charged with dissolved minerals assisted by compaction caused the sand to rapidly lithify. The beds of limestone, clays and silt (and coal) are the result of floodwaters washing over the sandstone as external forces lay siege to Earth.

Scant fossil evidence

Some scholars consider the Nubia (as most sandstones) entirely unfossiliferous whereas others would say "largely" unfossiliferous. This is due to the scant, if not debatable evidence. It is this we will take a look at next as the presence of even the most obscure trace fossils can be explained within the parameters of the ET model. It is essentially as we would expect.

> So far, the geological age of the formation remains enigmatic due to the failure of finding marine microfossils, particularly the index fossils. The sandstones previously dated as the Lower Cretaceous (Pre-Barremian) and Upper Jurassic based on the sporadic botanical and palynological data are generally uncertain and controversial. Marine microfossils, such as planktonic and benthic foraminifera, which serve as reliable tools in stratigraphic subdivision, have meagerly been reported during the latest three decades…
> http://www.micropress.org/micropen2/ articles/1/8/21751_articles_article_file_1820.pdf

The above paper by Jijun Zhang goes on to publish analysis results from core samples taken from two wells in the Gialo High of the Sirt Basin, Libya. It is beyond the scope of this book to comment on the specifics of the paper – suffice to say that some samples collected from this low-lying area show signs of marine fossils: "Almost all samples contain silicified marine microfossils, ranging from rare to common in abundance except for a few barren samples from the Upper Nubian Sandstone and Middle Shale." Also:

> In general, in the Upper Nubian Sandstone, fossils are rare or absent. For example, the lower part of core 1 of Well I is dominated by anhydrite microcrystals without microfossils. In the Middle Shale, fossils are more common and diverse with significant fluctuations. Microfossils are usually smaller in size than those recovered in the sandstones. The Lower Nubian Sandstone is dominated by large-sized trochospiral foraminifera.

When taking into account the quantity of sand falling over such a vast area – it would be reasonable to assume that some of this *must* have fallen in low-lying coastal areas and shallow seas – regions teeming with life where, as above, their calcareous remains would fall to the seabed and mix with the falling sand, creating nearshore sediments similar to that observed today. That is, up until the sand quite literally choked these areas.

The above study offers corroboratory support for this very simple sequence of events. Firstly, the samples taken are from a low-lying area, a basin (hence, the name Sirt Basin). A region no doubt subjected to marine waters and a place where we would expect to find fossil evidence – and that's exactly what we find. Secondly, the core samples reveal fossils are rare or absent in the upper layers whereas the lower layers seem to be dominated by large-sized fossil foraminifera. Setting aside the flood-borne shale deposits, this is consistent with sand choking what was originally a marine environment. Marine waters probably washed over low-lying areas quite regularly so as to fill or partly fill a channel, valley, sink or other depression – allowing life to take a brief hold before being swamped by extraterrestrial sand. I would expect any future studies to support this.

Furthermore, it is quite possible that temporary freshwater lakes (playas), ponds, rivers and streams (interior streams?) were created as water from outer space fell to Earth during this time – freshwater fossil evidence in support of this may one day be discovered. I would also strongly suggest that some fossils (including shells and organic matter) actually originated from Mars. All are possible, as there are obviously many combinations to consider here, but let us make one thing abundantly clear: the Nubia, as with the Navajo, the Coconino and many other sand and sandstone deposits are predominantly unfossiliferous, this is a fact. This doesn't bode well with the uniformitarian model of a slow and gradual accumulation of sand over billions of years in any environment. It does however, synchronise well with the ET model.

To sum up, it was the speed and intensity of the falling sand that made it impossible for life to remain or take hold in most regions. This is the primary reason why evidence for ancient life is so absent in nearly all sandstones.

FIFTY SHADES OF SAND

A quick internet search reveals that all of the aforementioned quartz-rich sand and sandstone formations display a range of colours from white to deep red and include yellows, reddish yellows, browns and buff. For example, the Saharan and Arabian deserts are mainly yellow and red. Depending on the light, dune sands can change colour from yellow to orange and red. Some of the reddest sand in the world can be found in the dunefields of the Simpson Desert in Australia and the coastal desert of south-west Africa, the Namib Desert. Most sandstones exhibit similar colours; the Nubian Sandstone, for instance, is most commonly brown or reddish, but in places it shows a much wider variety of colour. Similarly, the Navajo Sandstone exhibits a variety of colours from shades of red to stark white. Depending on where you look these can be quite striking, as in the image below. Somewhat unusually, the Coconino is typically buff to white in colour.

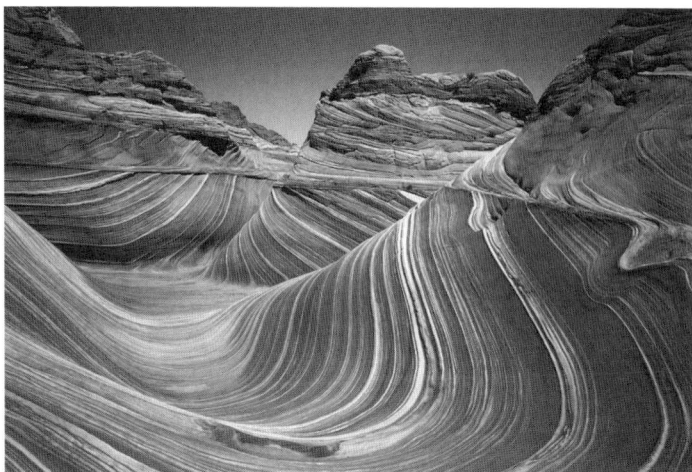

"The Wave." An area of fantastic, eroded Navajo Sandstone featuring beautiful swirls, striking colours (browns, beiges, yellows and buffs), countless striations, and bizarre shapes set amidst the dramatic surrounding North Coyote Buttes of Arizona and Utah. Wind-driven sand dunes laid down over millions of years or a more recent ET deposit? Where did the colour originate, above or below?

Source: http://en.wikipedia.org/wiki/The_Wave,_
Arizona#mediaviewer/File:TheWave_1600pixels.jpg

How does sand get its colour?

Most sand grains are coated with a thin glaze (varnish) of iron-rich clay minerals; it is this that gives the sand (and sandstone) its colour. It is a very similar chemical reaction to that of a rusting nail. An iron nail appears silver in colour and metallic. When a nail rusts due to the addition of water molecules and oxygen, two or three iron electrons are lost to oxygen (the iron is oxidized). The remaining electrons, together with the oxygen, absorb all of light's colours except red and brown. Essentially, the varying degrees of this 'rusting' process are responsible for the variety of colours found in sand and sandstone. In environments of high energy (i.e. beach sands) this varnish can be washed off to reveal the true colour of the quartz grain, which is in most cases clear with a yellow tinge. The colour is thought to be due to various impurities such as iron within the quartz.

It should be blatantly obvious by now that when it comes to sand nothing is straightforward; this would include the colour of sand, which is embroiled in controversy. All agree the colour derives from the "staining" of individual grains but there is no consensus of opinion as to how or where this originated.

> In addition to bright-yellow colours, the most widespread colour in desert environments is red. Field investigations have shown that red colour in desert sands is caused by the presence of hematite (iron oxide) coatings on individual grains. Reddened sands have been observed in deserts throughout the world, but their mode of formation is a matter of controversy.
> Farouk El-Baz, http://www.bu.edu/remotesensing/files/pdf/174.pdf

The source of the redness in dune sands puzzled early workers, who noted that it could not have come from within the sands themselves, which were largely quartz.

Desert Geomorphology. Cooke, Warren, Goudie, 1993 p.314

Not only is there little research involving the nanoscale characterization of coating mineralogy, but also the formation mechanisms of these coatings are poorly understood.

http://indiana.edu/~hydrogeo/Penn,%20Zhu%20 et%20al-2001-Geology.pdf

The most detailed study of stained quartz sands has been done in Australia. Sands from beaches in south-eastern Australia revealed (by examination using a scanning electron microscope) that the hydrated iron oxide (goethite) coatings were adhering not directly to the quartz grains, but to a submicroscopic clay coating. It was found that the clay coatings are a co-requisite for iron staining. In fact, they found no instances where an iron stain on a quartz grain consisted of solely iron oxide. In other words, quartz grains are first coated in a thin film of clay and adhered to this is the iron oxide – the iron oxide cannot exist without the submicroscopic clay coating the iron oxide cannot exist without the submicroscopic clay coating.

Source: Iron Staining of Quartz Beach Sand in south-eastern Australia. Sullivant, Koppi. pdf. 2006.
http://journals.fcla.edu/jcr/article/view/80685/77867

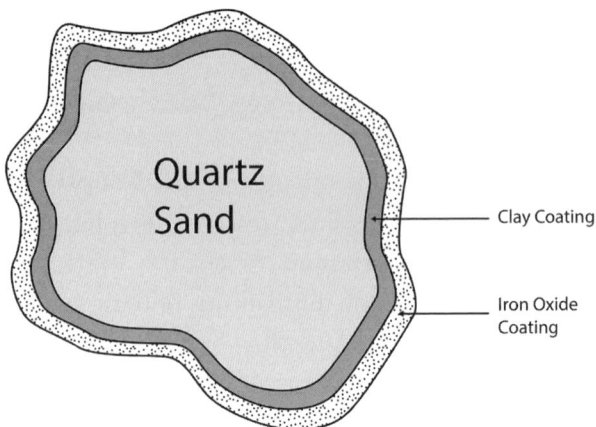

A typical Quartz grain with a primary submicroscopic coat of clay followed by a veneer of iron oxide.

When considering how quartz grains are supposedly born from granite the problem of coatings is an obvious one. Inasmuch as the quartz crystals in typical granite rock can be seen with the unaided eye, they take on a translucent greyish colour – the colour probably due to their immediate surroundings as the grains are essentially clear. They do not take on a reddish hue and are most definitely not coated in iron-rich clay minerals. Since granite is an igneous rock and as clay minerals can only form in the presence of water, it would actually be impossible for clays to form under these conditions, let alone coat individual grains.

Furthermore, the so-called "rock cycle" designating millions of years of weathering, erosion and transportation by rivers and subsequent deposition along the shore would have the effect of thoroughly washing the grains. It would not wrap them in a coat of varnish! Erosion by water in any environment will effectively bleach the sand. This means that it is *impossible* for any "first phase" (from granite) deposits of quartz sand to be coated in iron-rich clays – a very important point. With this in mind, just how (or where) did our "naked" grains of sand gain their coatings?

> The redness in an aeolian sand may derive from the parent sand (an already red alluvial sand or, more rarely, one with minerals which supply iron when weathered), from infiltrating waters, or perhaps most commonly, from dust added to the soil surface (walker 197, Wasson 1983a, Pye 1983h). Some authorities have found that source is the most important control on colour (Anton & Ince 1986).
> (Desert Geomorphology. Cooke, Warren, Goudie, 1993 p 316)

As we so often find, the majority (if not all) of sand and sandstone deposits are purported to be the result of multiple recycling events over millions of years and the suggestion that the redness derives from the "parent sand" is yet another example of this. Placing the problem way back in antiquity tells us nothing! It doesn't explain where the sand originated nor how the grains were initially coated in clay and then iron oxide. Where is this parent sand? Are there any remaining deposits and if so, how were they coated? Let's take an educated guess, the parent sand owes its colour to its parent sand, which in turn owes its colour to its parent sand… and so on, and so forth with no explanation as to the primary origin of the coatings, or even the genesis of the sand for that matter. Even if such multiple recycling events were in some way to blame, it makes little sense because each cycle would again thoroughly wash the sand, stripping it of its coatings. That would mean the grains must have been recoated many times over, but how?

If quartz grains were covered in a single mixed coat of iron oxide and clay (as originally believed) then some of the ideas forwarded by scholars may have some merit, but as the studies in Australia show, this is clearly not the case. Quartz crystals have two submicroscopic coats: a primary coat of clay and an outer rim of iron oxide, the former a co-requisite for the latter. This really is the crux of the matter and any model has to successfully account for this relationship. With this mind-set, we can see how the suggestion that the redness derives from "infiltrating waters" or "dust added to the soil surface" doesn't even come close to explaining how the two coats formed.

What procedure first extracts submicroscopic clay particles (mud) and then iron oxide from infiltrating waters or surface dust? How long does it take for grains to become coated? Are we looking along the lines of the uniformitarianism stance of billions of years, or perhaps just a few hundred thousand years? Any abrasion by wind or water "cleans" the sand so it stands to reason any accumulation would have to remain in a pretty stable environment for the coatings to take hold – but what sort of time period? Does one coating take longer to adhere than the other? Do the iron pigments wait around in the wings for tens of thousands of years before being allowed to adhere to the clay particles? Are there any deposits today in the process of gaining their first or second coat? Once the grains are coated would any subsequent water or dust yield further coats of clay or iron oxide? If not, and all the evidence seems to support this, why not? Actually, this would be impossible, as any iron staining would have to be removed first to allow the clay particles to adhere directly to the quartz grains. This strongly suggests a one-off initial event – but what?

If the processes in the rock cycle are correct then where are the "first phase" uncoated sand deposits? When considering the many millions of cubic kilometres of "virgin" sand that is supposed to have eroded from granite rock there should be tons and tons of primary sand. Added to this, the supposition that this is an on-going perennial cycle, we would expect to see copious amounts of "virgin" sand in and around the mouth of rivers and streams but this is clearly not the case.

The fact is that high-energy environments for the most part also contain coated grains, which again are believed to be the result of recycling. This is supported by the fact that the Australian samples were taken from a beach location. Also, preliminary examinations of the iron stains on quartz sand taken from rivers, soils and sandstone in the hinterlands adjacent to the coastline of the study area indicate that they have a similar mineralogy and micromorphology to those found in the beach sand.

This has led the authors of the study to propose a terrestrial origin for the colour. Prior to this it was generally thought the colour was the result of either a subaerial weathering of sediment exposed on the continental shelf during periods of lowered sea level, or from a subaqueous staining mechanism (source; Iron Staining of Quartz Beach Sand in Southeastern Australia. Ref. above). That being said, we're none the wiser as to what said writers mean by "terrestrial origin".

But if there are no deposits of virgin sand to be conclusively linked to granitic sources and practically everything we see today derives from recycled material, i.e. sandstone => sand => sandstone => sand, etc., then where does that leave the rock cycle? Have the processes of the rock cycle ceased? No, of course not. As demonstrated earlier the so-called rock cycle hasn't ceased so much as it just never got going in the first place. The whole concept is seriously flawed – it doesn't work and the problem of "colour" further highlights yet another reason why.

Let us for a moment imagine that divine intervention somehow played a part here and created an environment whereby earth's rivers and streams remained virtually unchanged for billions of years. In other words, no Milankovitch cycles, no glacial and interglacial periods, no tectonic activity and no sea level fluctuations – nothing to prevent the gradual build-up of substantial accumulations of virgin sand at the mouths of rivers, streams, along the shore, low-lying depressions, etc. (because this is exactly what it would take). Then what? After being deposited at the mouth of a river and along the shore, what happens next for sand to gain its coatings? One would assume it was blown inland but what would follow?

This very question can be applied to many of the aforementioned sandstones – a prime example would be the "Jurassic-age" Navajo Sandstone, its sand apparently born from granitic sources in the eastern US (Appalachians) and transported thousands of miles via an imaginary transcontinental river system and deposited somewhere in the west. Location, unknown – the evidence, non-existent... So keep imagining! It is said the sand was then blown from this unknown location to where it lies today, in the vicinity of the Colorado Plateau – where it formed vast accumulations of dune sand which over time became buried and lithified, and this is what we see today – sandstone that was once a colossal sandy desert as evidenced by displaying classic wind-blown features such as large crossbedding (as with many other sandstone layers found in the Colorado Plateau, such as the Coconino).

The question is, at what point during its journey did the Navajo sand become coated and how? Due to its high-energy birth and transportation it would be logical to assume it must have been post depositional but not according to some geologists.

> The sand dunes first piled up in the Jurassic deserts some 180 million years ago. The sands were red when they accumulated, and reddening continued for tens of millions of years during burial, compaction and cementation to form rock.
> Mysteries of Sandstone Colors and Concretions in Colorado Plateau. Chan. Parry. http://geology.utah. gov/online/pdf/pi-77.pdf

Since geologists are short of answers, a somewhat vague, sweeping statement is the best we can expect. Stating that the sands were already red when they accumulated does not explain the origin of the coatings, it merely pushes the problem back into obscurity – it formed elsewhere way back in time. Are we looking at recycling yet again? Was every last grain of sand removed from a previous accumulation? If so, where's the evidence? Certainly not recorded in the strata.

The same authors say having begun life as red sand, the wide range of colours comprising the Navajo today reflect a long history of alteration by groundwater and other subsurface fluids over the last 190 million years. They suggest different grain sizes in the strata also played a part in determining colour. This is perplexing in that if the sand originated from the same source then where did the different size grains come from? Shouldn't they all be roughly the same size? Time to add another few million years into the equation!

While I recommend reading the brochure, "Mysteries of Sandstone Colors and Concretions in Colorado Plateau", I believe there is little to be gained by discussing it in any detail. I think the best way forward would be to extract some of the main points and ask a few basic questions. From this we will see just how implausible the whole groundwater model sounds.

Question: how does groundwater (fluids) produce such defined alternating colours like those seen in "The Wave" in the image above? Consisting of intersecting U-shaped troughs that have been eroded into Navajo Sandstone, some of the laminae are virtually white; they are said to have been bleached by water, i.e. subsurface water has dissolved and removed nearly all of the hematite (iron coatings) and bleached red sandstone to white. How is that possible?

How does seeping groundwater (no matter what it consists of) manage to create such defined layers of bleached white sand the same time as creating interceding layers of red/brown/tan? Considering how some of the laminae are only a few inches thick, this has to be impossible. If anything, what we would expect to see is bleached whitish sand at lower levels merging into redder sand as we ascend (bit like rising damp) with the evidence obvious for all to see. This is clearly not the case with the Wave or the Navajo sandstone in general – or for that matter, the majority of sandstone formations worldwide. This can be seen by stepping outside the Wave and taking a look at some of the other outcrops.

Navajo Sandstone frequently occurs as spectacular cliffs, cuestas, domes and bluffs rising from the desert floor. It regularly overlies and interfingers with the Kayenta Formation (believed to be an ancient river deposit) of the Glen Canyon Group. Together, these formations can result in immense vertical cliffs of up to 2,200 feet (670 metres). Atop the cliffs, Navajo Sandstone often appears as massive rounded domes and bluffs that are generally white in colour. I refer the reader to the brochure where many of these can be seen, or a simple internet search. Comment: what a geological mess!

How does subsurface water manage to bleach vast quantities of sandstone so high up? Let us remember these formations are ancient wind-driven sand dunes frozen in time – they were all once apparently red. Even allowing for uplift, twisting, folding and weathering it makes little sense. Take, for example, the large outcrop in Zion National Park (south-western Utah) on page two of the brochure. Here we see that the upper Navajo Sandstone is mostly white with shades of yellow sitting on a reddish base (or parts thereof). Shouldn't it be the other way round? Shouldn't the base be white, blending into shades of original red as we move up through the ancient dunes? What of the shades of yellow? Again, as with the Wave, how can water be so discriminate?

There are many other similar formations where red layers and/or "blotches" of red sandstone can be seen scattered randomly among some extremely large bleached white mountainous outcrops. And then there's everything in between with some outcrops predominantly shades of red with lesser white segments. It is a chaotic mix with no obvious pattern – no two outcrops seem to be the same. In regard to colour it is virtually impossible to draw conclusions on one outcrop and compare it to another. The fact is if the consensus view is correct then some extraordinary random and selective bleaching on a gargantuan scale has taken place. Given the behaviour of water this is a highly implausible scenario no matter how you look at it.

Is this an on-going event? Is groundwater today anywhere on Earth selectively "bleaching out" sections of sandstone thus creating a similar chaotic mix of colours to that seen in the Navajo? We recall the world's largest known fossil water, the

Nubian Sandstone Aquifer System (NSAS), located in the eastern end of the Sahara Desert. Is the water here bleaching layers in a similar fashion? Highly unlikely considering it is used for agriculture and drinking water.

The most basic logic of common sense tells us it would be impossible for subsurface fluids to create such contrasting layers. It may further redden (oxidise) already red sands or even cause some bleeding of colour (this no doubt probably occurred), but not bleach them. High-energy environments bleach sand not seeping groundwater. This isn't to say that water in one form or another hasn't played a part in the Navajo, it undoubtedly has. We will discuss this shortly.

The best example of the shortfalls pertaining to the groundwater model can be seen by revisiting the supposedly 280-million-year-old Coconino Sandstone. We recall how this vast unfossiliferous sea of buried sand dunes covers an area of at least 518,000 square kilometres (200,000 square miles) across the Colorado Plateau. Containing a *minimum* of at least 41,700 cubic kilometres (10,000 cubic miles) of wind-blown sand it is comparable to the buried Navajo desert. It is also believed to have the same source as the Appalachians in the east. However, unlike the many colours exhibited by the Navajo, the Coconino is an unusual buff to nearly white. (Note: this author is unaware of any detailed petrographic studies done on the Coconino.)

Near white Coconino Sandstone. The cross-bed structure indicative of lithified desert dunes clearly visible.

Source: Wikimedia commons.

The first question that jumps out is what happened to its colour? Why nearly white? If subjected to the same basic processes (i.e. a fluvial origin followed by aeolian deposition) as the Navajo sand then where are the shades of red? Groundwater must have been present at some point since it assists in the cementation process but are we to believe fluids bleached white an entire 10,000 cubic miles of quartz sand over an area of 200,000 square miles? Of course not, it would be absolutely impossible to bleach such quantities so uniformly over such a vast area (it stretches from Arizona all the way to Canada), so there is little point in pursuing this avenue.

There is only one obvious and plausible explanation and that is the Coconino must have been white/buff prior to deposition. With that in mind and as improbable as it sounds, are we looking at the largest accumulation of first-phase quartz grains on the planet? In the conventional sense this raises a host of questions many of which we have covered before such as where's the primary source rock? What happened to the 168,000 cubic kilometres of mud (shale) produced during the weathering of the source rock? Where was the sand first deposited before been blown to its current location? Where's the evidence? And so on.

The deposition of such colossal volumes of pure quartz grains in one basic location would require an extremely stable environment lasting for many millions of years. In other words, there can be no Milankovitch cycles, no glacial and interglacial periods, no tectonic activity and no sea-level fluctuations – nothing to interrupt the formation of this vast desert. Was this the case? The evidence would suggest so since the strata of the Coconino records no such "climatic" events – it is essentially pure quartz. This once again deems the consensus model seriously flawed and unworkable.

In the same vein, how can a colossal sandy desert laid down over many millions of years manage to remain so pure in colour? Modern deserts such as the Sahara and Arabian deserts exhibit a variety of colours (brilliant white to dark red, pinks and oranges) and these are considered to be the "norm". So, what is so special about the Coconino? Similarly, some scholars (El-Baz) have suggested that dune sand reddens over time, i.e. the redder the dunes the older they are. Again, this clearly isn't the case with the Coconino – its lithified dunes are devoid of red sand. A most unusual situation, especially when considering how underlying the

Coconino is a layer of water-deposited mud (the reddish-brown Hermit Shale) and above is the Kaibab Limestone, also formed in water. On the subject of water, most of the layers in the Grand Canyon are said to have formed under water; with so much water around we may wonder how the Coconino managed to remain buff-coloured for 280 million years?

All things considered, if subsurface fluids were in any way whatsoever responsible for the coatings on individual grains then why can't scientists reproduce this in the laboratory? After all, it should be a relatively simple experiment that would go something like this. Ingredients: quantities of washed quartz sand in addition to samples of both white (Coconino?) and red sandstone (from anywhere) and water-based "fluids" (mud?). The experiment: using whatever fluids and processes scholars consider to be responsible, take the quartz grains and attempt to coat them. We are looking for *anything* even remotely resembling the Australian studies which show the coatings to consist of iron oxide adhered to a submicroscopic clay coating adhered to the quartz crystals (the clay coatings a co-requisite for iron staining). If laboratory experiments cannot achieve this, why not? Similarly, take the sandstone samples and endeavour to coat the white grains of the Coconino red or bleach the red sandstone white. Objective: by any means possible, attempt to replicate what we see in the field such as the striking coloured layers seen in the Navajo Wave. If unsuccessful, why?

I would like to make a very confident prediction: any experiments based on the current paradigm will *never* be successful, even if you add a gazillion years into the equation. The reason for this? Sand is extraterrestrial and it gained its coatings (or lack thereof) as it fell to Earth.

Electroplated desert sands – a form of plating

Every object has a net charge. That net charge can be positive, negative or zero. Quartz grains are considered as having a negative surface charge whereas clay minerals in most soils are positively charged. Iron oxides are also generally negatively charged, although the charge can vary.

Precipitating out of a moisture-laden, dust-filled atmosphere, immense clouds of sand fall to Earth – their size largely dictated by the density of the silica-based rock vapour. As the angular grains fall their surfaces take on a negative charge. Submicroscopic clay particles and iron oxides in the atmosphere become positively charged. Like a magnet, the negatively charged quartz grains attract the positively charged clay and iron oxide nanoparticles, coating the grains all over. This fundamental process (and the many possible variants) lies at the heart of how sand gained its coatings, indeed its colour.

The clay particles may have first adhered to the quartz grains as a result of being higher in the atmosphere followed by the attraction of iron oxides at lower levels. It may also be that once the hydrous (containing water) clay film formed, it allowed iron oxides to accrete or condensate on the surface of the grains. Another idea would be the iron oxides took on a negative charge as opposed to a positive one and these were attracted to positively charged clay particles.

Since clay minerals are hydrous aluminium phyllosilicates with variable amounts of iron, water (in the form of vapour, ice or liquid) also obviously played a part. It may be that the grains crystallised in the presence of water vapour – or with more certainty, fell to Earth encased in a thin film of water containing said clays and oxides (maybe organic matter as well). This way the grains would act as nuclei for water droplets. By way of analogy, let us take a look at a few "clouds".

Nocticulent Clouds (NCLs)

Night shining or Noctilucent Clouds (NLCs) are an unusual and intriguing phenomenon of the Earth's upper atmosphere. They form at the edge of space 83 kilometres above our planet's polar regions in the mesosphere. Seeded by "meteor dust", which forms the nucleus, NLCs (also called Space Clouds) are made of tiny ice crystals that glow electric blue when sunlight lances through their cloud-tops – they can also appear red and green. NLCs are generally only visible on rare occasions in the late spring to summer months in the hours after sunset and at high latitudes – 50° to 70° north and south of the equator. It should be pointed out that the mesosphere is the same layer where, as previously discussed, space debris oblates to re-condense and form meteoric smoke particles (MSPs), the precursors to grains of sand. However, the "meteor dust" referred to here is debris thought not to have vaporised. That said, scientists could be wrong and there may well be a direct connection.

Noctilucent Clouds. What would our ancestors have made of them? The distinctive ripples look like waves on a celestial sea. The Sun God Ra is often pictured as sailing the heavens in a "solar barque". Perhaps the celestial ocean was visible at lower latitudes due to layers of dust and debris hazing the sun red?

Source: Wikimedia Commons.

Although scientists are pretty sure meteoric dust provides the nuclei, the water vapour source is not known with certainty (Wiki). Most models, however, predict a terrestrial source – which is perplexing when considering how every day, earth is bombarded with more than 100 tons of cosmic dust, including cometary debris. Are we to believe none of this is water? I strongly doubt it. It used to be thought that water was very rare in the cosmos but actually we are starting to find it everywhere we look. Water is on other planets, it's on other moons and there are even asteroids with lots of water (more recent research indicates the asteroid Vesta once had water).

I am reminded of the late Louis A. Frank (1939–2014), a retired University of Iowa scientist, who along with his UI colleagues analysed data from the NASA satellite Dynamics Explorer I in 1981. Frank et al. concluded that as many as 25,000 small comets disintegrate in Earth's atmosphere each day (they also impact the Moon). Louis Frank was shamelessly ostracised for his findings and debate over his work still rages on. I concur with Frank's conclusions and would further suggest the comets are the last vestiges of Mars' missing oceans – still falling to earth along with dust and debris. More than that, extraterrestrial water provides an obvious source for NLCs.

Louis Frank's small comets:
http://smallcomets.physics.uiowa.edu/
http://sdrc.lib.uiowa.edu/preslectures/frank99/
page4.html

What the above gives us is a process whereby even today extraterrestrial material is falling to earth encased in water. A similar process is proposed for our grains of sand, i.e. microscopic water-bearing minerals attracted and adhering to the surface of recently formed quartz grains.

A very similar nucleation process also exists in the troposphere – the lowest layer in the atmosphere and where weather occurs. Studies here reveal mineral dust also plays a key role in cloud formation and chemistry at this layer. Moreover, it would seem dust particles are a necessary atmospheric ingredient in cloud formation.

> An interdisciplinary team from MIT, the National Oceanic and Atmospheric Administration (NOAA), and elsewhere has identified the major seeds on which cirrus clouds form. The team sampled cirrus clouds using instruments aboard high-altitude research aircraft, analyzing particles collected during multiple flights over a nine-year period. They found that the majority of cloud particles freeze, or nucleate, around two types of seeds: mineral dust and metallic aerosols.
> http://newsoffice.mit.edu/2013/cirrus-clouds-mineral-dust-0509

The nutrient-rich mineral dust is for the most part terrestrial in origin. The Sahara provides a major source, which subsequently blows across the Mediterranean (where it is the origin of rain dust) and Caribbean seas into northern South America, Central America, North America and Europe. It also plays a significant role in the nutrient inflow to the Amazon rainforest, so much so that without it the rainforest wouldn't survive (see: "Could the Amazon rainforest be only a few thousand years old?" on my website). I would actually argue that atmospheric dust in general must contain a good proportion of extraterrestrial material otherwise the question arises as to the whereabouts of the 100 tons of meteoric dust falling to Earth daily.

Be that as it may, once again what the research clearly shows is that cloud nuclei, even at lower levels, are microscopic dust particles that attract water vapour – and the whole point of the last few paragraphs has been to demonstrate how the same phenomenon gives us the means by which quartz grains gained their coatings. It was a combination of electromagnetic forces and vapour rich in clays and oxides individually coating the grains as they fell to Earth.

As with grain size, there are many variables to consider here: atmospheric moisture content, fluctuating levels of oxides and clays, "adhesion" rates, temperature, wind, etc. (in regard to temperature it should be pointed out that small water droplets can remain in liquid form in temperatures as low as -30 °C http://www.metoffice.gov.uk/learning/clouds/what-are-clouds). All this, and more, played a part in determining the colour of the sand grains. In short, it is envisaged that a moisture-laden atmosphere produced redder grains, whereas dryer settings gave rise to little or no coatings, resulting in virtually colourless grains (Coconino). And then there's everything in between dictating the variety of colours seen represented in quartz sands and sandstones worldwide. Although further research is required here let us now see just how easily things literally fall into place.

The most common colours – shades of red, brown and tan – were created in mainly wet environments. Some grains fell to Earth enveloped in raindrops, and this would further aid in the lithification process to form sandstones similar to the "Nubia". Other clouds of sand saw their mineral-rich water casing evaporated before settling on Earth. These are to be associated more with dune sand such as the "recent" deposits of the Sahara and Arabian deserts, or possibly the earlier solidified wind-blown dunes of the Coconino and Navajo. The variety of colours (and sizes) found in both dune sand and sandstones were due to changes in the atmosphere. Sometimes the colour variation was subtle as seen in many sandstone outcrops. Other times, it manifested itself in striking coloured layers like those of the Navajo wave (image above).

The *origin* of the colour (or lack thereof) will *never* be found in any geologic process – atmospheric processes dictated the colours observed today. This isn't to say post-depositional processes did not play a part (and continue to do so) in altering the colour of the sand. On the contrary, it would be foolish to suggest otherwise. Water in particular played a pivotal role. For example, rainwater, moisture, floodwater or groundwater would lead to further oxidation – turning red sands even redder and other sands a shade "richer". It would also bleach sand in high-energy environments (beaches, rivers). It would not, however, be responsible for the individual coatings of the grains; this was preordained by events in the heavens.

Take the case of the vast Nubian Sandstone complex. Although in places it exhibits a wide variety of colours it is most commonly brown or reddish. This is confirmed by the extensive outcrops located in the eastern Sahara, Israel (Amram Columns) and Petra in Jordan. The reader's attention is drawn to the sandstone cliffs in Petra in the image below.

Uneishu Tomb, the ancient city of Petra, Jordan. Just one of many awe-inspiring monuments cut into Nubian Sandstone cliffs. Note the horizontal layers running through the sandstone.

Source: Bernard Gagnon, Wikimedia Commons, http://commons. wikimedia.org/wiki/File:Uneishu_Tomb,_Petra.jpg.

Of interest here is the sandstone rock from which Petra was carved. Although better viewed online and in full colour I can confirm the colours here are arranged in layers that are essentially shades of brown and tan. They are most noticeable to the right of the picture and are typical of Nubian Sandstone in the region. Some "bleeding" of colour can be seen running down some of the rock faces; these streaks are to be ignored as they are caused by later flash floods prone to the region (an example of post-depositional processes at work). The bands or layers offer yet further support for the notion that the "Nubia" was laid down in one gigantic accretion event.

Upheaval in the solar system (impact on Jupiter or possibly a glancing blow to Mars by Comet Venus) caused unfathomable quantities of rock vapour to fall to Earth and recondense (as sand) covering an area of roughly four million square kilometres – the Nubia is born and earth grows a little! It shows shades of the same basic colours (despite being 3,000 metres thick in places) because it was laid down in one fundamental event lasting just a few decades if not less. The varying colours represent slightly different phases of the same event – dictated by variations in atmospheric conditions. It may well be that a slight change in temperature was enough to alter the colour.

The bulk of the "Nubia" fell encased in water droplets – creating some very wet sand, hence no evidence of windblown dunes. It probably also rained down in areas of shallow water adding to an already aqueous environment. A combination of incessant periods of deposition, burial and compaction provided the ideal conditions for rapid cementation. The interceding layers of clay and shale found in the Nubia are the product of floods and tsunamis washing over the increasingly hardening sandstone (much of this also originating from Mars).

The consensus of millions of years played no part here. If it did the colour of the sand wouldn't be so thick and consistent in places. What we should be seeing is a 3,000 metre unconsolidated mix of clays, shales and sand along with an *abundance* of fossil material. This is especially so when considering how the Nubia is said to have been deposited in a shallow marine environment. Now, just exactly where are those fossils?

Most sandstones (and sand) were laid down in a similar fashion to the Nubia. The ancient Coconino desert (and other similar buried dunes), on the other hand, provides us with an excellent contrasting variable. Its brilliant white sands reveal they were set down in a mainly dry environment where little in the way of coating took place – an atmosphere virtually devoid of clays and oxides, thus preventing the "plating" process from taking place. Perhaps the temperature somehow prevented adhesion? Perhaps the atmosphere contained iron oxides but for some reason the essential primary clay coating wasn't initiated and this prohibited the build-up of oxides? Maybe future petrographic studies will show some of the Coconino grains to have the thinnest of coatings (submicroscopic?) and this being the reason for the observable shades of yellow. Who knows? There are many things to consider. However, one thing is for sure, the sands comprising the Coconino were not "bleached" so much as they were never coated in the first place. Certainly not enough to turn them red no matter how many millions of years you ascribe to them.

The Navajo was laid down in a similar wind-borne fashion to the Coconino, that is to say any moisture had largely evaporated prior to deposition and this is why the Navajo also bears the hallmarks of an aeolian desert. But the Navajo presents us with a much more colourful pallet than the mainly white Coconino. In fact, the Navajo displays the widest range of colours seen in any sandstone. This tells us that conditions in the atmosphere underwent rapid changes in a relatively short period of time. The striking colours seen in the "Wave" are a perfect example of this. The almost white bands represent phases of little moisture and adhesion (analogous to the Coconino grains) while the tans and reds denote varying degrees of moisture and oxidation. The thin and colour-contrasting stratified sequences (sometimes only a matter of inches thick) are indicative of the rapid atmospheric changes which occurred – a thin band of virtually white sand could easily be followed by a thick brown layer, and so on and so forth. And all within just a few days, if not hours.

Subsequent uplift and water erosion (floodwater, groundwater) may have twisted and carved out gullies and canyons but the colours were predetermined by conditions above. Groundwater also probably assisted in the rapid lithification of the Wave (and the Navajo in general) as I doubt very much that the sand was subjected to the action of the wind for an extended period of time. If it were laid down over millions of years as per consensus the layers wouldn't be so defined. The sand would be more mixed as opposed to looking as though its strips were "frozen" in time. The latter totally consistent with catastrophe and the ET sand theory.

RAPID DEPOSITION – A SNOW CANYON AND A SAND CANYON – A BRIEF ANALOGY

Image inside Wire Pass slot canyon. The primary entrance to Buckskin Gulch, Vermilion Cliffs National Monument in southern Utah, USA.

Source: Jason J. Corneveaux, http://en.wikipedia.org/wiki/ Buckskin_Gulc.

Not far from the navajo Wave we have the Wire Pass slot canyon, a tributary to Buckskin Gulch, the longest slot canyon in the world. The Wire Pass is made from Navajo sandstone. It was formed, as most canyons, by the wear of water rushing through through the rock. The walls can reach heights of 30m (100 feet) and less that one meter (3 feet) across. There are many similar canyons cut from Navajo sandstone in the region. Note the many hundreds if not thousands of wind deposited layers, the colours of which are largely tan or brown. About halfway up the walls we also have what appears to be a watermark or two. Was this near pristine unfossiliferous quartz sand the result of millions of years of weathering, erosion, and deposition, or as proposed, an accretion event lasting just a mattter of months or years? Is there amything to compare it to? I believe there is.

Yuki no otani (Great canyon of snow) on the Tateyama Toll Road, Tateyama Town, Toyama Prefecture, Japan.
Photograph by Uryah @ Wikimedia Commons

The Tateyama Kurobe Alpine Route is an international mountain sightseeing route some 90 kilometers (56 miles) long. The route goes across the 3,000-meter-high North Alpine mountains, the so-called 'roof of Japan,' and connects Toyama and Shinano Omachi. You can enjoy the panorama by taking a train, highland bus, trolley bus, cable car, and ropeway. Since the lines opened in June 1971, the Tateyama mountain area has been transformed from an isolated spot into one of the nation's best sightseeing areas, where a million guests visit every year.

Murodo-daira of Tateyama has one of the heaviest snows in the world, and the snow reaches about seven meters (23ft) on average. In particular, the snow mantle at Otani, a five-minute walk from Murodo Station, sometimes gets more than 20 meters (65.6 feet) because of snowdrifts. The famous "Snow Walls" are formed by expelling this heavy snow, and the 500-metre-long area with such snow walls is open to sightseers from mid-April to late May. (Source: Japan National Tourism Organization.) Note the many hundreds of snow layers made visible in Japan's snow corridor – these aren't unusual. Dig a hole in any snow with a depth of only a few centimetres and you should be able to observe snow layers. They can even be seen on a roof (side-on view). They form over the winter season; the snowpack typically accumulates and develops a complex layered structure made up of a variety of snow grains, reflecting the weather and climate conditions prevailing at the time of deposition as well as changes within the snow cover over time.

The analogy is an obvious one, the 65-foot snow layers bear a striking resemblance to the Navajo sand layers. The reason for this is just as obvious – they were both laid down rapidly. The snow layers in just a few months, the layers of sand a similar timescale, if not slightly longer. Both rained down from above, the multiple overlaid layers corresponding to particular sand and snowfall phases. The main difference between the two would be post prepossesses (i.e. freezing, thawing) were much more involved in shaping the snowfall phases. Altering the texture and probably levelling them out more (snow metamorphism). The tough quartz sand deposits far less so – the coloured layers haven't altered much since they were laid down.

In summary, the many enigmas surrounding the origin of colour fade away once we adopt the ET sand theory. A prime example of this would be the aforementioned Australian studies – which show that samples collected from the beach, river, soils and sandstone, were all found to have similar mineralogical and micromorphological properties. An impossible situation given the contrasting environments and consensus logic. A much more straightforward answer would be that the iron-stained sands bear many similarities because they originated from the same extraterrestrial source. The sand fell from the sky in just one of many very recent sand accretion episodes (in the last 3,000 to 4,000 years). They maintain their iron-rich coatings as a direct result of their recent deposition. Not enough time has elapsed for weathering and erosion to have had a discernible effect.

Impurities and colour

The apparent colour of a mineral can vary widely because of trace impurities or a disturbed macroscopic crystal structure. Small amounts of an impurity that strongly absorbs a particular wavelength can radically change the wavelengths of light that are reflected by the specimen, and thus change the apparent colour. Coloured diamonds contain impurities or structural defects that cause the coloration, while pure or nearly pure diamonds are transparent and colourless. Quartz sand also contains impurities, namely iron oxide. This can also have an effect on the apparent colour of sand. Thoroughly washed grains (i.e. no coatings) can appear yellow due to traces of iron. The tiniest impurity can affect the colour – consider a drop of ink in a bucket of water – enough to colour water and similar to what impurities can do to minerals.

Quartz sand (silica) is the main raw material in commercial glass production.

Early glass derived its color from impurities that were present when the glass was formed. For example, 'black bottle glass' was a dark brown or green glass, first produced in 17th Century England. This glass was dark due to the effects of the iron impurities in the sand used to make the glass and the sulfur from the smoke of the burning coal used to melt the glass.

In addition to natural impurities, glass is colored by purposely introducing minerals or purified metal salts (pigments). […] Sometimes it is necessary to remove unwanted colour caused by impurities to make clear glass or to prepare it for coloring.

http://chemistry.about.com/cs/inorganic/a/aa032503a.htm

Where did these impurities originate?

It stands to reason that if sand formed in the skies above then any impurities must have also been present during this time, and this is exactly what I propose. The rock vapour from which vast swathes of desert sand condensed, also contained impurities. These trace elements remained as the quartz crystals formed – precipitating with the quartz. I consider this to be the natural order of things – it's what would happen if said thesis is correct. After all, impurities such as sodium (Na), Iron (Fe), potassium (K), magnesium (Mg), Calcium (Ca), in addition to various other oxides, are all present in the mesosphere. As we have seen, along with silicon vapour, they form Earth's "Atomic Metal Layers".

THE MARTIAN MANTLE – THE ULTIMATE SOURCE OF QUARTZ SAND ON EARTH

The majority of sandy deserts consist almost entirely of quartz grains (>90 per cent), the remainder largely feldspars. There are exceptions. For example, sand collected from the Namib dunes (Sossus formation) showed the sand to be composed of only 46 per cent quartz with the remainder feldspars and rock fragments. However, in most cases, quartz dominates. The same applies to sandstone deposits – quartz is by far, the dominant mineral, e.g., Nubian, Coconino and Navajo. The question is why? Why is quartz so dominant? If, as I have proposed, sand is the result of 3,000 to 4,000 years of planetary upheaval in the solar system, then why aren't we presented with a more mixed bag of minerals – a more balanced proportion of quartz, feldspars and other rock fragments? Additionally, the production of such vast amounts of quartz sand deems the atmosphere must have been absolutely saturated with virtually pure silica (SiO_2) – how is that possible? If extraterrestrial, where's the ultimate source?

Answering these questions requires taking a brief look at the structure of Earth and Mars and revisiting the almost incomprehensible birth of Mercury from Mars as set out in my "rough chronological order" section.

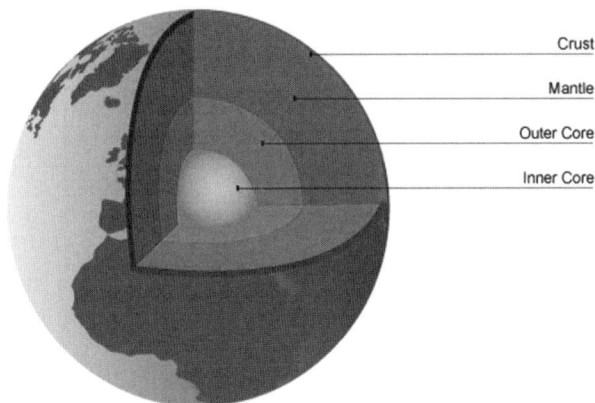

Cross section showing structure of the Earth.
Source: Wikimedia Commons.

The Earth is made up of four distinct layers:

1. The inner core is in the centre and is the hottest part of the Earth. It is solid and made up of iron and nickel with temperatures of up to 5,500°C. With its immense heat energy, the inner core is like the engine room of the Earth. It is thought the core spins faster than the rest of the planet and this acts as a dynamo (electricity generating) generating earth's protective magnetic field

2. The outer core is the layer surrounding the inner core. It is a liquid layer, also made up of iron and nickel. It is still extremely hot, with temperatures similar to the inner core.

3. The Earth's mantle is a layer with a thickness of 2,900 kilometres or 1,800 miles (46 per cent of the Earth's average radius of 6,371 kilometres or 3,960 miles) and extends from the outer core of the Earth at 3,500

kilometres radius from the centre of the Earth, to the lithosphere that is only less than 200 kilometres (124 miles) thick, so it constitutes about 86 per cent of Earth's volume. The mantle is thought to be semi-molten, becoming more molten towards the outer core. It is composed of silicates.

4. The crust is the outer layer of the Earth. It is a thin layer between 0 and 60 kilometres thick. The crust is the solid rock layer upon which we live. More than 90 per cent of the crust is composed of silicate minerals, the most abundant of which are feldspars (60 per cent).

Of particular interest here is the composition of Earth's mantle.

The exact composition of the mantle is not known with certainty, but is determined or inferred by the material coming from volcanic eruptions coming from up to 300 km depth. It is concluded by now that the composition of the mantle is 46% silicon oxide, 38% magnesium oxide, 8% iron oxide and other compounds like 'garnet.'
http://www.artinaid.com/2013/04/composition-of-the-earths-mantle/

The 46 per cent silicon (silica) presents a bit of a problem for scientists in that it seems there isn't enough silica when compared to that of their apparent meteoritic origin.

Earth's upper mantle is apparently depleted of silicon when compared with meteorites, which are thought to

represent the material from which the Earth formed. This 'missing silicon' problem has provoked intense debate: it suggests that the deficit might be balanced by silicon in the core, or that the upper mantle is not representative of the entire mantle and that the lower mantle is enriched in silicon. Murakami et al. provide evidence to support the latter case. They made laboratory measurements of sound-wave transmission through silicate perovskite and ferropericlase minerals at pressures and temperatures matching those of the lower mantle, and compared the resulting shear-wave values with seismic data that sample the lower mantle. They conclude that the mineralogical model that provides the best fit is one in which perovskite constitutes greater than 93% of the lower mantle. This suggests that the lower mantle is enriched in silicon in comparison with the upper mantle, consistent with the chondritic Earth model, and that there is limited mass transport between the upper and lower mantle. Earth science: Lower mantle may be rich in silica. Ian Jackson. Nature 485, 51–52 (03 May 2012).
http://www.nature.com/nature/journal/v485/n7396/full/485051a.html#access

This raises the question if free very dense silica polymorphs exists in Earth's deep interior. Although it is generally accepted that the SiO_2 component of the Earth's lower mantle occurs as $(Mg,Fe) SiO_3$-perovskite, recent experimental evidence for the dissociation of perovskite at about 80 GPa greatly increases the probability of free dense silica in the Earth's lower mantle.
http://www2.jpl.nasa.gov/snc/news31.html

The above experiments indicate that silica becomes more pure the deeper we travel towards Earth's core. A very important point, for need I remind the reader that quartz grains are nearly all pure silica or silicon dioxide (SiO_2). This means that Earth's mantle has the potential for providing an endless supply of quartz grains. Indeed, if only a small fraction of this were present in Earth's atmosphere as a vapour there'd be more than enough (being the largest part of the Earth's volume) to create every single grain of sand on the planet an infinite number of times over. Actually, we're not that far off from what occurred, only earth's mantle played no part here – it is the silica-rich mantle of Mars we turn to for the ultimate source of earth's sand deposits.

Although less is known about the composition of Mars, orbiting spacecraft, landers and analysis of Martian meteorites have confirmed it to be very similar to Earth.

> Mars is a terrestrial planet, which means that its bulk composition, like Earth's, consists of silicates (minerals containing silicon and oxygen), metals, and other elements that typically make up rock. Also like Earth, Mars is a differentiated planet, meaning that it has a central core made up of metallic iron and nickel surrounded by a less dense, silicate mantle and crust. The planet's distinctive red colour is due to the oxidation of iron on its surface.
> (Composition of Mars, Wiki)

But this is today, a somewhat far cry from my proposed "Earth-like" in every sense. Let us proceed with that in mind.

Mars – once so similar to Earth, apart from size, it would be very difficult to tell them apart. Far from being the red planet, the spacecraft Voyager 1 would see them both as "Pale Blue Dots". The similarities would extend right through to the composition, in that Mars was also home to a rotating solid iron core powering a protective magnetic field. Surrounding this we have the liquid iron/nickel layer followed by the thick mantle and the outer solid rock layer, the crust (where humans like you and I once lived). The mantle, as with Earth, would make up the bulk of the planet and consist of similar silicates – which, again like Earth, would become more pure in silicon as we descend towards the core. This is the region where most of Earth's quartz deserts began life – as silica-rich Martian magma. The question is, how do we get rock from deep within Mars to Earth? Answer: it was sucked out along with the Martian core!

Disturbed from its orbit by the initial explosion on Jupiter and later possibly sideswiped by the resulting newly formed Comet Venus – Mars enters into hundreds of encounters with Earth (and Venus). The "Earth–Mars battles" continued for centuries (Egypt's Pharaonic battles) and culminated in the iron heart of Mars being ripped out through the Valles Marineris to become the "iron" planet Mercury, or as the Ancient Egyptians initially called it, the Aten ("The Disc of the Sun", a dazzling orb in the image of the Sun). An apocalyptic event that (as you would expect) also saw large volumes of residual iron/nickel "droplets" and staggering quantities of molten silica sucked up from deep within Mars and violently flung out into space – large proportions of silica (and iron) vaporising in the process. Many of these glassy silicon clouds made the relatively short journey to Earth (we will discuss how and what form this may have taken shortly) to ultimately precipitate out of the atmosphere as quartz grains. This is the source of the virtually pure sand deposits on Earth – the virtually pure silica from the depths of the Martian mantle.

Recalling any of the aforementioned sand or sandstone accretions, if they comprise almost exclusively of quartz grains then they originated from the silica-rich Martian mantle, especially the more recent deposits like the Sahara and Arabian deserts. They contain little in the way of precipitated feldspars as a direct result the deconstruction of Mars from deep within.

If correct, then it stands to reason that Mars should be home to some virtually pure silica deposits. It may lie hidden beneath the largely basaltic surface to perhaps outcrop in certain areas, nevertheless it has to exist. Is there any evidence for silica on Mars? Absolutely!

NASA's Curiosity Mars rover has found a target unlike anything it has studied before—bedrock with surprisingly high levels of silica. Silica is a rock-forming compound containing silicon and oxygen, commonly found on Earth as quartz. July 24, 2015 "NASA's Curiosity rover inspects unusual bedrock."
http://phys.org/news/2015-07-nasa-curiosity-rover-unusual-bedrock.html

At the time of writing, the above was breaking news. Scientists were so *surprised* by the find they backed up the rover 46 metres to for further investigation. I predict other high-silica areas will be found if not by the Curiosity rover then by future probes.

Explaining the feldspar content

Although rare, some sand deposits exhibit a much lower ratio of quartz to feldspars. Consisting of only 46 per cent quartz with the remainder feldspars, the dunes of the Namib Desert are a good example. How is this explained?

Although the genesis of Mercury was a one-time event the whole process was played out over millennia – it was all part of the slow and systematic destruction of the once Earth-like Mars. What this means is prior to and for many centuries after giving birth, Mars convulsed and ejected many hot bodies (iron and rock) and vaporised material into space, not just from the region of the Valles Marineris. Indeed, induced by highly transient alignments with other bodies (hence the ancients fear of eclipses) hundreds of volcanoes erupted and appeared to spit "fire and venom" as they "lashed out" into space. The surface of Mars quite literally boiled as streams of lava snaked across its surface (such traits are what gave rise to the Egyptian cobra). A cauldron of catastrophe, all of which provided an endless mix of rock vapour.

Now, as you would expect, the composition of this vapour was determined by the type of rock vaporised, i.e. mantle rock, as we have seen, produced a silica-rich gas. Surface or crustal rock, on the other hand, consisting of more felsparthic material (as with Earth), naturally produced a vapour rich in feldspars. This is the primary origin of feldspar grains in sand, and littered about the earth for that matter. It derived from the vaporisation and ultimate precipitation of surface rock as opposed to mantle rock.

Is there evidence for feldspars on Mars? If I am correct there should be ample quantities, or evidence thereof.

For a number of years now Mars has been considered to be geologically rather simple. The surface was thought to be almost entirely dark-coloured volcanic basalt. The primary constituents of which are olivine, pyroxene and plagioclase feldspar – that is to say, little in the way of the more common feldspars like those found in granite. However, in 2012 the Mars rover Curiosity sampled soil, which yielded data suggesting that there may be more to Mars than just basalt.

Spectral characteristics of the Mars soils resemble those previously reported for feldspar-rich lunar anorthosite (a feldspar with a chemical composition – $CaAl2Si2O8$) but the Mars samples are accompanied by 'secondary alteration products' namely, clay minerals. This is not what scientists expected or predicted. Indeed as James Wray, the lead author of the recent Nature Geoscience publication explains: 'Using the kind of infrared spectroscopic technique we were using, you shouldn't really be able to detect feldspar minerals, unless there's really, really a lot of feldspar and very little of the dark minerals that you get in basalt'. The fact that no basalt was detected in

the location of the feldspar further supports the theory that the feldspar may be linked to granite.
http://www.rockcollector.co.uk/editorial1113.htm

Our finding of felsic materials in several locations on Mars suggests that similar observations by the Curiosity rover in Gale crater may be more widely applicable across the planet.
http://www.nature.com/ngeo/journal/v6/n12/full/ngeo1994.html?WT.ec_id=NGEO-201312

And more recent headlines… July 15, 2015:

- A home from home: Curiosity finds Martian crust that reveals red planet is far more like Earth than thought.
- Rock rich in feldspar, with what is believed to be quartz.
- Find is unexpectedly similar to Earth's granitic continental crust.
- http://www.dailymail.co.uk/sciencetech/article-3161511/A-home-home-Curiosity-finds-Martian-crust-reveals-red-planet-far-like-Earth-thought.html#ixzz3fx4kN0Eo

In short, the discovery of felsic outcrops (and feldspars in general) on Mars are leading scientists to believe there may be an abundance of feldspars below its largely basaltic surface. Unlike scientists, this author is not surprised by these findings. They are consistent with the ET theory that Mars once had a feldspar-rich crust, however post-apocalyptic (post birth of Mercury) erosion, sedimentation and volcanism have subsequently erased any clear surface evidence for widespread felsic materials.

Any vapour from Mars would of course mix together. Indeed, along with impurities, Earth's atmosphere would play host to a rich blend of silica and feldspar vapour. The ratio was dictated by events on Mars – Mercury's birth combined with incessant internal convulsions deemed this to be silica dominant with lesser amounts of feldspars. Or to put it another way, we have small quantities of surface rock mixed in with large quantities of mantle rock so to speak.

We can see how this manifested itself by merely taking a look at the precipitated sands on Earth. For example, we have seen how virtually all dune and lithified sands comprise largely of quartz grains with a small percentage of feldspars. This simply tells us that although most of the material originated from the mantle, small quantities were the result of boiled surface rock. Sands exhibiting higher levels of feldspars indicates crustal rock played a more significant role. It really is a simple as that – the many compositional variations merely reflect the type of rock blasted off or excavated from Mars.

It is with ease we now explain the high levels of feldspars and rock fragments (approximately 55 per cent) comprising the Namib Desert. They are a direct result of an accretion event that involved the vaporisation and subsequent precipitation of enormous amounts of both crustal and subsurface mantle rock. This fell to Earth and what we see today is exactly what we'd expect to see – quartz mixed in with substantial amounts of feldspars and bits of rock.

Let us remember such proportions of feldspars shouldn't exist if the consensus model of weathering and erosion from granite is correct – they should have been washed away in solution to form clay minerals in the very first instance. They exist because the rock cycle is in serious error – there was no gazillion years of weathering and erosion of inaccessible granite prunes, no repeated recycling events (which would only further dissolve feldspars), just vast clouds of sand raining down on earth in one of many sand phases.

We recall Mars' North Polar Basin (Borealis basin), which falls to a depth of 6 kilometres and covers a whopping 40 per cent of the planet. Planetary scientists suggest that the basin was formed by a mega impact. But if this is so then where's the physical evidence for the composition of the projectile? More importantly, what happened to the countless tons of material supposedly excavated by such an event? Vanished without a trace? Thrown out of the solar system? Highly unlikely.

The North Polar Basin was shaped as Mars entered into many encounters with Earth. The gravitational forces of Earth quite literally excavated and sucked up tons of volatiles, dust and debris from Mars' northern hemisphere as its north pole tilted towards Earth. Hence, no evidence for an errant body.

Mars' north Polar Basin here filled in with water (large dark patch) to gain an idea of the material excavated from this region.
Source: Wikimedia Commons.

The reason for mentioning the Polar Basin is because it probably played a significant part in the creation of the Namib Desert. For a start, the removal of any crustal rock no doubt involved the vaporisation of tons of feldspar-rich material. Now, mix this with silicon-rich sub-surface rock and we have the basic ingredients for the Namib sands. Another combination may well be that crustal rock from the northern regions combined with vapour from the Valles Marineris region and this gave us the Namib – both are possible. One thing I am fairly sure of is that the North Polar Basin formed after the birth of Mercury. The loss of Mars' core meant the dismantling of its protective magnetic field thus allowing the total depletion of Mars' northern regions. By this logic the Namib isn't the oldest desert in the world as per consensus – it is one of the youngest!

Given the dynamic nature of the proposed events, there is nothing extraordinary here, it is as expected given the many variations of the ET sand model. If a body of sand contains a large percentage of quartz grains then its source lies with the Martian mantle. If however, feldspar grains dominate, then we look to the crust of Mars for the source. And then there's everything in between, but the very fact that quartz is the dominant mineral in most sands and sandstones tells us they originated from deep within the Martian mantle. This may not be an exact science but the basic principles are there.

A cautionary note: as mentioned previously, I'm not ruling out the newly formed Comet Venus as a potential source of rock vapour – I am sticking with Mars because it is missing a great deal of material. As I said in my previous books, Mars, the great warrior god king was seen to be constantly at war as it was systematically torn apart whereas Venus, in total contrast, essentially cooled down – it was rarely (there were occasions!) observed in battle. And as such, was naturally associated with a more passive divine queen than a warrior god king.

Left: Sahara desert. Right: the surface of Mars. Both worlds bombarded by rocks and sand.

Source: NASA.

The flight from Mars – two phases?

Mars, an incandescent fiery red orb looming larger than the Sun (Re) during ancient historical times. A scalding hot body spewing out untold volumes of rock vapour (SiO) over several millennia, large clouds of which fell to Earth. The question is, what form did this take before encountering Earth? Did silica enter Earth's upper atmosphere as a gas, or something more solid?

There were probably at least two phases (or stages) of vaporisation and condensation of Martian rock. The first phase: trillions of tons are vaporised and flung out into space (along with hot flying lava). This rapidly solidifies in the cold of space to form dense interstellar clouds of microscopic glassy particles or spherules. While the majority of these fall back to the surface of Mars to be reassimilated, many glassy clouds are drawn towards Earth. Stage two sees the spherules once again vaporise as they enter earth's atmosphere. They are no match for Earth's defensive shield – instant vaporisation. A thick dense layer of rock vapour builds up – quartz and feldspar grains precipitate, crystallize and rain down on Earth. Variables apart, this is the most likely scenario.

As we have seen, silica (SiO_2) exists in many different forms that can be crystalline as well as non-crystalline (amorphous), or glass-like structure. It is difficult to envisage ejected silica vapour doing anything other than rapidly solidifying in such a cold environment (space -273 C). The silica vapour droplets would immediately freeze (technically, desublimate) into microscopic glass beads. In other words, no time for crystals to grow. An analogy would be Microtektites (or glass spherules), which are bits of glass formed from molten or vaporised Earth rock ejected into the atmosphere by cataclysmic impacts of comets or asteroids. The glassy matrix a direct result of rapid cooling.

Scolding hot rocky planets, vaporised rock and molten ejecta; is there anything to compare to? Fortunately there is. What follows is an article published by NASA in August 10, 2009. I have extracted some of the more relevant sections. It paints a good picture.

- Planet Smash-Up Sends Vaporized Rock, Hot Lava Flying
- NASA's Spitzer Space Telescope has found evidence of a high-speed collision between two burgeoning planets around a young star.
- Astronomers say that two rocky bodies, one as least as big as our moon and the other at least as big as Mercury, slammed into each other within the last few thousand years or so – not long ago by cosmic standards. The impact destroyed the smaller body, vaporizing huge amounts of rock and flinging massive plumes of hot lava into space.
- Spitzer's infrared detectors were able to pick up the signatures of the vaporized rock, along with pieces of refrozen lava, called tektites. The astronomers used an instrument on Spitzer, called a

spectrograph, to break apart the star's light and look for fingerprints of chemicals, in what is called a spectrum. What they found was very strange. "I had never seen anything like this before," said Lisse. "The spectrum was very unusual."

- After careful analysis, the researchers identified lots of amorphous silica, or essentially melted glass. Silica can be found on Earth in obsidian rocks and tektites. Obsidian is black, shiny volcanic glass. Tektites are hardened chunks of lava that are thought to form when meteorites hit Earth.

- Large quantities of orbiting silicon monoxide gas were also detected, created when much of the rock was vaporized. In addition, the astronomers found rocky rubble that was probably flung out from the planetary wreck.

- Spitzer has witnessed the dusty aftermath of large asteroidal impacts before, but did not find evidence for the same type of violence – melted and vaporized rock sprayed everywhere.

http://www.nasa.gov/mission_pages/spitzer/news/spitzer-20090810. html

Mars exhibited similar catastrophic traits to the recently discovered "planetary wreck", except that Mars was torn apart by on-going planetary encounters as opposed to any bull's-eye impact. We have everything you would expect to see from a rocky body in absolute turmoil – vaporized rock, hot flying lava and an abundance of glassy material. The orbiting silicon monoxide (SiO) is interesting in that Mars must have been home to something very similar, as volatiles, dust, debris and tons of rocky vapour orbited around its girth.

A visual analogy would be Saturn and its rings, only thicker and denser (in previous works I have compared this to the design of the blue Egyptian war crown). I would take this one step further and suggest there were many periods when the whole body of Mars was enveloped in a seething mix of rock vapour and volatiles. The rock maintained in a gaseous form due to the extreme temperatures. In this state Mars periodically appeared as an incandescent red orb with a thin yellow encircling "atmospheric" vapour band or rim – *exactly* as represented in the infinite but erroneously labelled "sun discs" of the ancient Egyptians. More on this later.

Logically, the chemical composition of any vapour, glassy material or otherwise depended on the type of rock vaporised, and with this comes the many variables as discussed. However, since mantle rock has a higher silicon dioxide (SiO_2) content than crustal rock, and as most sand on Earth is quartz dominated, we can deduce that even though large quantities of mantle rock were ejected out into space via the Valles Marineris, most of the surface vapour must have remained on Mars. This is anticipated seeing as it would require a substantial amount of force to escape the gravitational pull of Mars. In addition to this, the production of rock vapour was a continuous process during heightened periods of chaos. This is not to say it didn't happen. On the contrary, the very fact that Mars has had its top "blown off" is evidence of one immense and lengthy 'surface' extraction event. Only when planetary chaos subsided and Mars cooled down somewhat (thus creating less rock vapour), was the solar wind able to fully strip any vestiges of volatiles, dust and debris out into space. Leaving Mars in a condition not to dissimilar to what we see today.

Is there any evidence whatsoever for the first phase? I believe there is.

Glass dunes on Mars and the Moon

In 2012, The European Space Agency's Mars Express orbiter revealed that up to *10 million* square miles of volcanic glass sand cover the surface of the Red Planet.

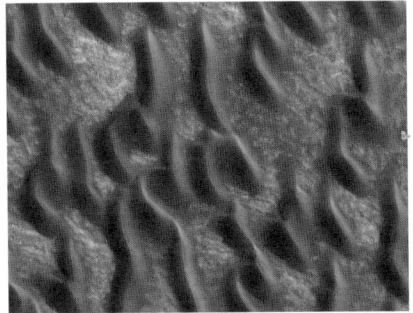

Left: Dusty, glass-rich sand dunes like these found just south of the north polar ice cap could cover much of Mars. Right: The north polar sand sea and the Acidalia Planitia (the large, dark region near the top) of Mars are primarily composed of glass.
Source: NASA

Dark patches visible across much of the northern Martian hemisphere aren't canals or vegetation, as once thought, but volcanic glass according to a new study. Using near infrared spectroscopic data collected by the European Space Agency's Mars Express orbiter, Horgan and Bell found widespread weathered volcanic glass covering the surface of the Martian lowlands:

"The glass is most likely volcanic glass produced during explosive eruptions, and potential sources include volcano-ice interactions in the northern lowlands," say researchers Briony Horgan and James F. Bell of Arizona State University. "The glass deposits also exhibit signs of weathering, indicating widespread interactions with liquid water."

"The volcanic glass (probably basalt) was created when hot magma reacted explosively with ice or water," says Horgan. "The same sort of thing happens in Iceland, where volcanoes erupt under glaciers. The interaction with the ice and the water causes the magma to become super-explosive, creating tonnes of sand sized black particles."

"These form vast sand dunes covering about a quarter of Iceland's surface, which is exactly what we're seeing on Mars," says Horgan. "We see these dark plains and enormous glassy sand dune fields up in the northern Martian polar regions."

"This is the first direct evidence on Mars for explosive volcanism on a planetary scale."
Source: http://m.space.com/15484-mars-volcanic-glass-life.html

Although originally thought to consist of typical iron rich basalt (as most surfaces on Mars) a new spectral investigation of the glass sediments (by the same scientists Horgan and Bell) has now revealed that they are almost entirely composed of iron-bearing glass i.e., largely silica with iron. (http://www.psi.edu/pgwg/images/jun12image.html)

It will be shown here how the vast deposits of glass sand dunes on Mars are consistent with the ETS model. They are the result of a logical order of events and provide evidence for phase one glass. The key here is Martian "rain" which came in many forms.

Prior to, during and for many centuries after Mercury's birth, Mars internally and externally convulsed. Its surface boiled and thousands of volcanoes violently erupted sending plumes of lava, rock vapour, dust and debris high into the Martian atmosphere – some out into space en route to Earth. But that's only part of the story; Mercury's exit also saw the creation of iron droplets (chunks) of various sizes in addition to countless tons of iron vapour – which combined with the rock vapour to form a thick, dense iron-rich rocky atmosphere.

In an almost perpetual cycle large quantities of rocky vapour condensed and rained back down to the molten surface where it was either swallowed up, blasted back into the atmosphere or revaporised. "Hell on Mars" would be an understatement! Driven by turbulent storms, this was a nightmare world where a mix of rocky material rained down on Mars for millennia. Is it any wonder all signs of life have been obliterated?!

The Martian "rain" took on many forms including that of molten droplets, glassy beads (tektites) right down to minute glassy particles analogous to the iron-bearing sediments observed today. Unlike Earth, which saw the relatively slow precipitation of quartz grains, most Martian rain manifest as a glass due to rapid cooling.

Its composition depended largely on the schedule of events. For instance, prior to and post Mercury's genesis would see more in the way of a basalt (low silica content) – very similar in composition to the volcanic crust covering most of Mars today. In contrast, Mercury's birth created vast amounts of more pure silica rain – the primary source of Earth's deserts as quantities were ejected into space. The same period also no doubt witnessed iron vapour solidifying and raining down on the surface as iron rain.

I am reminded of failed stars known as brown dwarfs where temperatures are so hot it is thought iron rain is commonplace (http://www.space.com/24192-stormy-weather-brown-dwarfs-aas223.html). Something similar must have occurred as Mars gave birth to Mercury. A global event that led to the formation of the iron rich basalt covering most of Mars.

As to be expected, some vapours mixed together – forming a variety of silicate glasses – some rich in iron, others less so. The evidence for these phases has all but disappeared, assimilated by oceans of molten magma – that is, with the exception of the glass in the northern lowlands (and, as scientists are now discovering, many other locations). Having done a little groundwork, it's now possible to explain how these formed.

Planetary chaos receded, Mars began to cool, its volcanoes became less active and its birth scar (VM) began to heal – the manufacture of rock vapour dwindled. Even so, vast clouds of glass particles, dust and debris remained scattered throughout the solar system and in orbit around Mars (and Earth). Over time these rained down on a solidifying surfaces – this being very close to what we see today – vast oceans of iron bearing glass sand covering almost a third of the planet. We are essentially looking at the legacy of one of the final phases in the demise of Mars and the production of sand.

The composition of the glass (iron bearing) poses a problem for scientists as it is unlike the iron-rich basaltic crust covering most of Mars. The ET model suffers no such qualms – the glass consists largely of amorphous silica and iron because it was ejected from the Valles Marineris region – a place where mantle rock mixed with iron from the core of Mars.

The beauty of the theory is that even if future studies reveals compositional variants to that observed today, the theory simply moves with it. For example, higher readings of basalt denotes more surface rock melt, whereas higher concentrations of iron indicates an increase in iron vapour, and so on and so forth. The fact is, where scientists struggle to provide answers the ET sand model naturally incorporates any variables.

Some interstellar glass clouds may have remained in space for many decades – before ultimately being swept up by a rapidly cooling Mars (and the other planets). We may compare this to Earth's orbit intersecting the path of meteor showers such as the Perseid and Leonid meteor showers (both the legacy of earth Mars encounters). However, as the Martian atmosphere dissipated (subjected to the full force of the solar wind), the glass rained down virtually unhindered, or at the very least, through an atmosphere that had little effect.

Another possibility is that Mars retained a rocky atmosphere during later times, presenting us with a similar process to that which occurred on Earth. That is to say, space-borne glass may have revaporised as it fell back to the surface of Mars. However, unlike the glass that fell to Earth and subsequently precipitated out as quartz crystals, Martian rain rapidly condensed back into glass particles. This being a direct result of having a different atmosphere – Earth, oxygen-laden replete with a magnetic field. Mars, on the other hand, laden with rock vapour and devoid of a magnetic field. Either scenarios, or a combination of both are possible.

Volcanoes in Iceland erupt underneath glaciers, and the interactions between water from the glaciers and lava from the volcanoes create incredibly explosive eruptions. The lava fragments, and transforms into particles of glass. Huge sand dunes and sand plain fields form that consist of 50 to 70 per cent glass. Horgan and Bell hypothesize that the same process occurred during periods of volcanism on Mars (ibid).

Setting aside the composition problem, other drawbacks exist with said thesis, not the least of which, there is just too much glass, it's too concentrated and unlike Iceland's volcanic glass fields, there's no obvious source. Light work is made of such problems with the ET model. The glass-rich sedimentary terrains are the result of glass sand raining down on the surface of Mars. We may compare this to quartz falling to Earth only on Mars where similar material fell as glass sand. The source lies with the creation of rock vapour on a planetary wide scale over several millennia. It could be said Mars was once one massive volcano as mantle rock was also drawn up from deep within the core of Mars. The glass show signs of weathering as water (acidic fluids) also fell back to Mars and along with extreme winds washed the glass particles into the low-lying areas where they remain today. It is predicted here that future space probes and or studies will support my whole stance by identifying further global deposits of "first phase" glass especially in low lying areas (VM?).

First-phase glass on the Moon as well?

Much of the composition and structure of the Moon is still a mystery to scientists – less than a quarter of its surface has been mapped in detail, and little is known about how it formed, what it is made of, and how it has evolved over time.

> Lunar soil is composed of various types of particles including rock fragments, mono-mineralic fragments, and various kinds of glasses including agglutinate particles and volcanic and impact spherules.
> http://en.wikipedia.org/wiki/Lunar_soil

Intense cosmic battles also saw the recently birthed Moon (from Jupiter) vacuum up countless tons of Martian debris as it slowly fell under Earth's spell. As with Mars, much of this was swallowed up (assimilated) by the Moon's molten surface over many millennia (imagine throwing a rock into a boiling hot lava pool). However, as chaos began to subside, the Moon began to cool and the crust and mantle began to harden. Continuing meteor bombardment and volcanism subsequently led to the formation of the lunar regolith, or soil.

The lunar regolith which is approximately 3 to 10 metres deep, consists of a jumble of large boulders, rocky debris mixed in with fine dust particles and of interest here, microscopic glass spheres, or spherules. Indeed, glasses are one of the main components of lunar regolith. They are thought to arise from micrometeorite impacts, as well as fire-fountain volcanoes – a process whereby volcanic lava is lofted and cools into small glass beads before falling back to the surface.

No matter how you look at it, there seems to be little doubt that the Moon's glassy material was created by impact-induced volcanism, or volcanism of sorts. But the question is, was it the result of volcanism on the Moon or first-phase glass ejected from Mars, or perhaps a combination of both? I naturally lean towards a Martian origin.

Origin Mars?

Although the Moon played a part, the bulk of the glass (and debris) comprising the lunar regolith was the result of intense volcanic activity on Mars. We are again looking at the latter stages of chaos – a time when errant planets began to settle into their present orbits and the Moon (Thoth) undertook the ceaseless task of clearing up glassy debris from Mars – thus clearing a path to the gods, the divine stars and the firmament beyond.

Unlike the rocky Martian atmosphere that may have revaporised any "phase one" glass as it fell back to Mars, the Moon was (during the latter stages), as it is today, effectively devoid of any atmosphere. This means that the glassy particles falling to the Moon, fell virtually unhindered. There was no burning up during decent – and this is what we see represented in a good proportion of the luna regolith today – a record of vaporised material ejected from Mars frozen in space and subsequently swallowed up by the Moon (and of course Earth).

Almost half of the Moon's glass consists of silicon dioxide (amorphous SiO^2) – a crucial ingredient in the production of quartz sand. Moondust is also rich in iron, calcium and magnesium bound up in minerals such as olivine, pyroxene and other trace elements. (http://science.nasa.gov/science-news/science-at-nasa/2006/30jan_smellofmoondust/.)

This is consistent with the striping of mainly felsparthic material from the Martian surface during the latter stages of Mars' demise.

The Moon?

The Moon has been pummelled by millions of impacts – there are impact craters everywhere, and the surface is completely covered with pulverized rock and ejecta. A cataclysmic event known as the Late Heavy Bombardment (LHB) about 3.9 million years ago is said to be responsible. It was a period of intense comet and asteroid bombardment that is thought to have peppered all the planets including the Earth. In keeping with the general theme of this book: the dates for the LHB are absurd – they record events (Pharaonic battles) of only a few thousand years ago, not billions. The primary source of the LHB was debris from Mars (and let's not forget, possibly Jupiter), which pummelled the moon incessantly. With this in mind it would be foolish to say the Moon didn't manufacture at least some glass.

Large chunks of rock (asteroids, comets) travelling at tens of thousands of miles per hour (with no atmosphere to stop them) hit the moon instantly vaporising the underlying rock sending plumes of lava and rock vapour many kilometres into space. Rapid condensation follows and clouds of glass rain down on the Moon. Such events undoubtedly occurred, but to what extent?

I strongly contend the bulk of the Moon's glass is first-phase glass from Mars. The main reason for this stance is the amount of glass and its relative uniform powdery texture – even when allowing for incessant bombardment, there is just too much of it. It virtually envelopes the whole body of the moon and it is much too fine and consistent. A problem recognised by planetary scientists that has led to the notion that micrometeorites (small metallic particles of iron) are responsible.

These *tiny* iron specs are thought to impact the Moon, thus vaporising the underlying rock and forming microscopic fountains of glass beads which fall back to the surface of the Moon. A process that is apparently not only still on-going but has continued for some billions of years. Indeed! This makes little sense given the fact that regolith covers almost the entire lunar surface and has the consistency of talcum powder (some say flour). It would be like throwing a grain of sand into a bed of talc some three metres plus deep. How would that produce a fountain of bedrock glass particles?

How do you access the bedrock with so much powdery material in the way? How on earth did the Apollo astronauts survive with such a barrage of deadly missiles flying around?

No matter what the velocity, the idea is seriously flawed, and yet the process is supposed to have occurred all over the Moon for eons. Could the process be reproduced in a lab environment? I strongly doubt we could get anywhere near what we see on the Moon given the current thinking. The reason for this is apparent – the glass has nothing to do with impacting micrometeorites – it is largely phase one glass, ejected from Mars and swept up by the Moon. If our recently captured moon hadn't vacuumed up the glass it would have eventually fallen to Earth providing yet further fuel for quartz sand. The glass didn't impact the Moon so much as make a soft landing – pretty much to be expected from microscopic dust particles.

Another good reason for pointing the finger at Mars is the composition of the glass grains

In 1993, Lindsay Keller and David McKay (Johnson Space Center) using transmission electron microscopy (TEM) found nanophase-sized metallic iron beads in silica-rich glassy rims on individual mineral grains in Apollo lunar samples. It is this so-called "nanophase iron" that led to scientists to come up with the micrometeorite impact theory in the first place.

Quoting on a TEM image of a glass particle from the moon:

> This ellipsoidal lunar glass particle contains numerous tiny spheres of nickel-iron. These metallic spheres are meteoric in origin and indicate that the glassy particle was produced by shock melting during a meteoric impact.
> https://airandspace.si.edu/exhibitions/apollo-to-the-moon/online/science/lunar-rocks.cfm

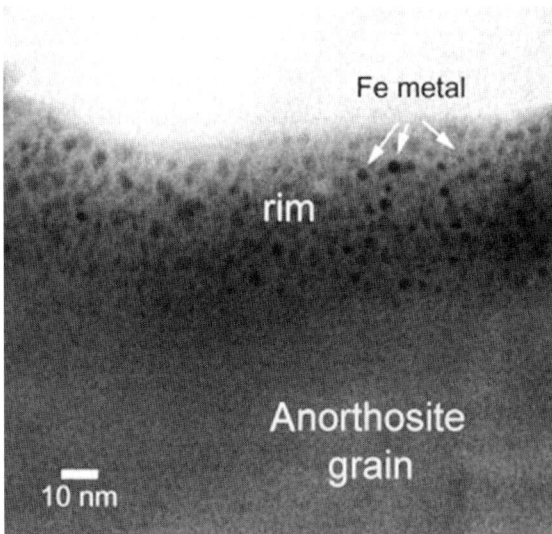

(From Keller *et al.*, 1999; Pieters *et al.*, 2000.)

Vapour-deposited Fe metal particles (Fe^0) in a SiO_2-rich glassy rim of anorthosite grain from a mature lunar soil. Virtually all grains of a mature mare soil (long exposed to space weathering) have such rims.

Source: Lindsay Keller (NASA), http://www.psrd.hawaii.edu/ July04/newMineral.html.

The consensus view in brief: miniscule grains of iron (mostly 10 to 150 micrometres) travelling at full cosmic velocity (20 or more kilometres per second – 70,000 to 150,000 km/hr) somehow bypassed 3 to 10 metres of regolith to impact the Moon's bedrock sending up plumes (again, bypassing layers as it rebounded) of iron and rock vapour that rapidly solidified to form minute glassy grains of rock coated with a mix of iron (Fe^0) and silica (SiO_2). Is it no wonder scientists are struggling with this one! Exactly how do individual anorthosite grains become coated in a silica-rich glassy rim containing nanophase beads of iron? Once again, Mars holds the answers.

As discussed, intense tidal heating caused the surface of Mars to periodically boil giving rise to an iron-rich silica based atmosphere. The moon glass analysed thus far derives from mainly feldspathic material that has condensed in such an atmosphere – Martian surface rock blasted out into space but not before being coated in a mix of silica and iron. When taking into account the consistency and staggering quantities of the glass I deem this the most logical explanation.

That being said, another possibility would be that "uncoated" first-phase glass particles ejected from Mars subsequently fell into a boiling hot Moon, which was similarly home to an iron-rich, silica-based atmosphere (origin, Mars). So, as the particles descended they became coated in a mix of silica and iron. In such a seething environment the particles may have re-melted as they fell and this may have assisted in the glassy iron garnish. What we have here is something analogous to the clay and iron coatings that formed around quartz grains falling to Earth. Perhaps it was too hot for the clay coatings to form hence just the iron rim. In simplistic terms, contrasting atmospheres would naturally give rise to a variety of coatings.

The glass on the Moon is essentially first-phase glass – it lies where it fell. It has nothing to do with "space weathering" (micrometeoritic impact theory), which makes little sense when considering the depth of the regolith. Had it have fallen to Earth it would have revaporiscd separating out into the different compounds – to eventually form (in this case) a mix of quartz and feldspar crystals (50 per cent?) containing iron impurities, or re-condensed "melted" iron micrometeorites. Using basic logic, we should consider the possibility that even today left over bits of micro glass particles are continuing to soft land on the Moon (and other planets including Earth), albeit on a very much diminished scale.

MICROMETEORITES (MMs) –
THE ON-GOING LEGACY
OF RECENT CHAOS

Please note: at present, the study of MMs is at best ambiguous, so what follows is more of an overview and nowhere near an in-depth study.

More than 5 to 400 metric tons of meteoric debris enters the Earth every day. Most of it in the form of small meteoroid particles with sizes smaller than 2 millimetres. These are called micrometeoroids. About 90 per cent of micrometeoroids totally vaporise upon entry to Earth's atmosphere. We have seen how the evaporated material forms Earth's metallic layers. The material re-condenses to form "meteoric smoke particles" (MSPs, the precursors to quartz grains) which ultimately rain out of the atmosphere. The surviving 10 per cent is commonly known as micrometeorites (MMs).

A micrometeorite is an extraterrestrial particle, ranging in size from 50 μm to 2 millimetres (smaller than a grain of sand) that has survived entry through the Earth's atmosphere. They account for 99.5 per cent of the extraterrestrial material falling on Earth's surface each year (mass = expanding Earth). Sometimes meteoroids and micrometeoroids entering the Earth's atmosphere are visible as meteors or "shooting stars,", whether or not they reach the ground and survive as meteorites and micrometeorites. MMs differ from meteorites in being smaller, more plentiful and different in composition and are a subset of cosmic dust, which also includes the smaller interplanetary dust particles (IDPs). The deposition of MMs can be found virtually anywhere; in desert soils, in beach sand, in glaciers – they gently land in our fields, on our homes, and on us. Step outside your door and you've probably stepped on a good number of micrometeorites, they are that common. (https://en.wikipedia.org/wiki/Micrometeorite)

Four textural types of MMs can be distinguished based solely upon how they have been heated (or not) entering the Earth's atmosphere. The four categories are: cosmic spherules (melted), scoriaceous (leftover from melting or boiling), coarse grained and fine grained (no evidence of melting).

Left: An assortment of melted micrometeorites: Light microscope images of stony cosmic spherules. Right: Highly friable fine-grained unmelted MM recovered from fresh snow in Antarctica.

Source: Hopson Road, Wikimedia Commons.

The mineral compositions of MMs have shown that they are related to both asteroids and comets. Many MMs have an array of minerals that look similar to carbonaceous chondrites (meteorites). The majority of these minerals are silicates and iron sulfides. (Source: https://catalyst.uw.edu/workspace/idp/40208/285084)

As stated so many times now the solar system is a smoking gun of recent planetary upheaval. Asteroids, comets, dust and debris are the leftovers of some barely comprehensible events. Included in this melee were MMs – minute stony and iron fragments ejected mainly from Mars in the last few thousand years.

Stony fragments

We recall the idea that close encounters with Earth caused the northern hemisphere of Mars to be excavated to a depth of some 6 kilometres (North Polar Basin) and how I place the said episode towards the latter stages of chaos – a time when Mars having already being stripped of its iron heart began to cool. Now, while some rock no doubt vaporised or turned to lava, comparable quantities (if not more) did not, and this is where we get the bulk of MMs. They are the tiny leftover fragments of rock sucked up from the Martian surface not initially subjected to melting.

I would suggest the source was highly friable sedimentary material – rock previously broken down into very small pieces as a direct consequence of swirling 300 mph winds, landslides, volcanic eruptions, mega earthquakes and tsunamis. All this and more, contributed to the production of cometary debris, rocks, stones, pebbles and micrometeoroids – large amounts of which were sucked up by Earth or thrown out into space. Countless quantities remain scattered throughout the solar system and continue to fall to Earth (and the other planets). The majority undergoing complete vaporisation, the remainder subjected to varying degrees of melting. The composition of stony MMs would depend on the type of rock excavated, so once again any number of variables are possible – which is what we find, an assortment of rock forming silicates.

Metallic MMs

Some MMs are made of iron or iron and nickel and can be collected with a magnet (see below on how to do this). The daily bombardment of iron debris comes as no surprise – it is as expected given Mercury's birth. I imagine a similar process to the formation of sand, i.e. masses upon masses of iron vapour rapidly condensing in the cold of space and forming minute iron-rich particles (beads?). They remain scattered throughout the solar system and are still falling to Earth to partially melt, vaporise completely or descend unmelted – although I'm none too sure about the latter. The ablation of iron-rich micrometeoroids (and iron meteoroids) is the accepted source for the iron in the mesosphere – which subsequently manifest as iron impurities and coatings in and on quartz.

Overall, the fact that silicate minerals dominate MMs with iron particles making up the balance (approximately 2 per cent) is consistent with mainly crustal rock (feldspars) mixed in with a little iron/nickel from Mars' core. I would also add, there is nothing primordial here, especially in regards to iron – all iron, from the smallest particle to the largest iron meteorite, has its origin in the Mercury from Mars event.

Iron coatings on MMs

Unexpectedly, all types of unmelted micrometeorites (UMMs) are coated with a thin partial or complete iron oxide coating (magnetite shell) which makes them highly magnetic (hence the name, magnetite). Although the process is poorly understood most agree the magnetite shell formed as a result of atmospheric entry. It is similar to fusion crusts found on meteorites and is seen as an extraterrestrial signature of a particle and probably required an oxygenic atmosphere

Source: M. Maurette. Micrometeorites and the Mysteries of Our Origins. 2006

The first thing that immediately jumps out here is that we have a process whereby descending particles are coated with iron oxide. It may be a poorly understood process; nevertheless, it is a process that occurs above our heads on a daily basis. There are obvious comparisons to be made here not least of which the iron coatings found on quartz sand. We recall how the red colour in desert sands is caused by the presence of hematite (iron oxide) coatings on individual grains and how I propose this occurred in the atmosphere. The coating of UMMs offers strong support for this. Indeed, it is pretty obvious a very similar process must have taken place.

UMMs are coated in magnetite (Fe_3O_4), whereas quartz grains have a hematite (Fe_2O_3) coating (with a base coat of clay). Magnetite and hematite are minerals of iron. Both have iron in different oxidation states, and they are in the forms of iron oxides. To turn magnetite to hematite essentially what is required is more oxygen. It is not too difficult to imagine how oxygen levels fluctuated widely during past periods of chaos. The extra oxygen probably came from the Martian atmosphere or water falling to Earth. Scientists do say that atmospheric oxygen levels were much higher in the past. Problem is, they're locked into the blinkered "millions of years" scenarios.

Things have settled somewhat and if grains of quartz were to condense out of the atmosphere today they may become coated in a similar iron oxide to MMs, or they may not. There are so many things to consider, such as the composition of the particles and the environment in which they fall. Let us remember, quartz grains have a thin coat of clay, a prerequisite for the iron oxide coating. Perhaps here, the water (H_2O = hydrogen and oxygen) in the clay assisted in oxidising the iron into hematite.

An example of how we're delving into unknown territory would be the question of why only UMMs display signs of an iron oxide coat – why don't all surviving MMs have similar coatings? Perhaps scholars have got this one completely wrong and there's no such thing as unmelted MMs and what we are observing is precipitated material developing an iron coat as it falls – very similar to the formation of quartz grains. It would certainly make sense in that how can such highly friable particles remain unmelted upon encountering Earth's atmosphere? You would think they would vaporise completely – perhaps this is exactly what is occurring.

We recall the glass particles on the Moon, which have a coating of iron as opposed to iron oxide. This tells us they either fell in or were created in an iron-based environment devoid of oxygen. If subsequent studies reveal the presence of iron oxides, it simple means the presence of oxygen. Again, the theory is flexible.

The consensus theory that the iron coatings originate from iron MMs can further be dismissed for the reason that the majority of MMs consist of silicates and not iron. What, we may ask, happens to all these as they pummel the moon? If they are devoid of iron where does the iron rim come from?

Total vaporisation

The majority of MMs (and IDPs) do not survive atmospheric entry; they evaporate completely and are responsible for Earth's metallic layers. They are the source of meteoritic smoke particles (MSPs) that literally rain out of the sky. Not surprisingly we have a composition analogous to surviving

MMs, i.e. largely feldspathic material with a small amount of iron – consistent with mainly surface rock excavated from Mars' northern hemisphere blended with residual iron from Mars' core.

This indicates there is little in the way of pure silica impacting the Earth today – any first-phase glass has long since been vacuumed up and apart from the glass on the Moon and Mars the evidence for the production of quartz grains has diminished. Indeed, even if we were to dramatically increase today's flux of MMs to the point of saturation, the composition is such that it would be largely feldspar grains precipitating out of the atmosphere, not quartz. However, if we turn the clock back to the time of Mercury's birth and the creation of masses of pure silica mantle rock – quartz grains would dominate.

Unlike today's MMs which reveal a small per cent surviving atmospheric entry, I have suggested that the majority of first-phase glass totally vaporised. The reasoning behind this is as follows. Quartz grains initially began life from the rapid condensation of silica-dominated vapour as it exited the VM region of Mars – vast clusters of microscopic glassy particles followed (phase one). The particle size was similar to that of MMs (50 to 100 μm size fraction?), however, the effect of desublimation (direct from a gas to a solid) meant that they were far more uniform and compositionally consistent (pure amorphous SiO_2). Smaller particles actually have a better chance of surviving entry (less surface area, less friction = less heat and less chance of burning up), which is why I have suggested a size comparable to that of MMs (since most of these vaporise). These basic traits (uniform size and composition) are the main reason for the total evaporation of phase one glass as it fell to Earth. The silicon gas subsequently precipitated out as quartz crystals (phase two) and created many a sandy desert.

In contrast, MMs originated from the highly friable feldspathic crustal rock and as such consisted of a variety of sizes and compositions. They probably experienced little or no thermal alteration until descending to earth where the majority then vaporised. That being said, minerals largely form by the crystallisation of magma or lava, so some primary heating obviously took place as the minerals naturally formed on Mars (igneous phase).

We are perhaps splitting hairs here for if we were to throw both MMs and the glass particles into the mix falling to Earth, all would be considered as MMs (technically micrometeoroids until they hit the ground). And this is indeed exactly what occurred during historical times. However, there exists subtle but noticeable differences between the two both compositionally and processes undertaken. One consisted of pure silica and experienced at least two phases of vaporisation/condensation. The other subjected to one vapour phase and comprised of largely feldspar material.

Past times saw a vast increase in the manufacture of both leading to an atmosphere super saturated with a mix of silica and feldspar vapours. The subsequent precipitated quartz to feldspar ratio depended on the composition of incoming material. As the sandy deserts reveal this was a quartz-dominated world.

In short, MMs on the whole are the microscopic legacy of recent planetary chaos, asteroids and comets being their larger cousins. They fell in vastly increased volumes during earlier times and are the source of feldspar grains in quartz sand (and around the globe). They no longer rain out of the sky because, as with quartz grains, the density is now insufficient. Providing a condensation nuclei for rain, they now fall to the surface of Earth as MSPs (begs the question, what would be the effect on rainfall without MSPs, would it rain as much?).

Footnote: Although I have suggested that interstellar glass clouds have all but disappeared, there is a strong possibility that some still remain. Further research is required here, especially in the field of interplanetary dust particles (IDPs). Who knows, future studies may perhaps one day find pure glassy particles in space. I can see the headlines now, "scientists were surprised to discover…"

In a similar vein, we should also be open to the possibility of quartz and feldspar grains precipitating out of the atmosphere today. Let me explain. Quartz and feldspar grains litter the surface of Earth; they can be found in most soils. I have personally filtered out many from common garden soil in the UK. As with MMs they are virtually everywhere. Indeed, MMs samples collected from the South Pole Water Well (SPWW, a 4000-cubic-metre subsurface water pool, Antarctica) also contain a large per cent of quartz and feldspars, but where are they coming from? They are presumed to be detrital (glacial debris) but where's the source? Sand grains are in general too large to be carried in true suspension by the wind so this rules out anything blown up from any sandy desert. What of the abundant grains present in soils throughout the world? Feldspars weathered from rock are said to form clay minerals – why haven't these turned to clay, especially as there're purported to be millions of years old? Similarly, if derived from glacial moraines how did they come to settle in the topsoil of my garden!

As I contend the majority of sand is extraterrestrial and the same applies here – the loose granules also derive mainly from above. However, the question here is did they fall to Earth recently, i.e. in the last few decades as opposed to millennia ago? Moreover, is it possible quartz and feldspar grains (and other stuff) are still precipitating out of the atmosphere? Has the density in some regions being such that MSPs have further grown into crystals? Is sand still raining down on us on a minute but daily basis? To date, I'm not convinced this isn't the case. An open mind is required but it would make sense when considering how Earth is blanketed by great quantities of loose granular material. Further research is required here.

Now, who wants a piece of Mars' core?

Tons of MMs fall to earth each day. Most are stony and are difficult identify but the metallic (iron/nickel) ones can be collected from almost anywhere in the world by using a magnet. I have included some very simple instructions on how to do this. I would advise all to try this. Its good fun and done correctly it will prove fruitful.

To collect micrometeorites you need to find a place where they can become concentrated. The drains of a house or building work well since rainwater can wash particles off of an entire roof and collect them at the drain spout. Tile roofs are best since they drain very well and do not produce many other sorts of particles or debris.

But dust, plants, pieces of window screens and all other sorts of airborne material also collect there. To find the metallic micrometeorites, collect and dry some of the material from a deep bowl at the base of the drain spout. After removing leaves and other debris, place the remaining material on a piece of paper and place a magnet under the paper. Tilt and tap the paper so that all of the non-metallic particles fall off. Many of the remaining metallic particles are pieces of space dust! To examine them, place the paper under a microscope. High power will be required to see them clearly. Most of the particles are not from space, but the micrometeorites will show signs of their fiery trip through the atmosphere. They will be rounded and may have small pits on their surfaces. Source: http://www.rockhounds.com/rockshop/micromet.html
See also: http://www.iflscience.com/space/how-hunt-micrometeorites

It is also possible to extract micrometeorites from desert sands or a beach. A strong magnet in a plastic bag is all that is required. Just pass over the dry sand.

If wet, dry out first (in a container) and then use the magnet.
http://www.instructables.com/id/How-to-Collect-Meteorites/

To retrieve from common soils you will first need to filter away all the organic material by washing (I used a stocking) under a tap. Allow the soil to dry and then use a magnet in a bag to collect as described above. Actually, I used the very same filtration method to disinter quartz and feldspar grains.

So what do you have with these iron-nickel specimens? The consensus view will tell you much of what you are observing are particles that date from the formation of the solar system around 4.6 billion years ago. I tell it differently… you now own a fragment of Mars' core!

THE ACCRETION OF SILICA
AND IRON DEBRIS

Predictably, Mercury's birth not only gave rise to vaporised material but also heaps of more solid material, notably variously sized chunks or droplets of pure silica and iron. By way of offering further support for the ET sand thesis I think it would be a good idea to take a look at some these, in particular silica droplets but first a brief word on iron meteors.

The iron-nickel droplets ejected from the Valles Marineris ranged in size from dust-sized particles to small "moon-sized: bodies (<50 kilometre diameter at a guess). Many of these fell back to Mars to be assimilated by its molten surface – others were scattered throughout the solar system. Some large droplets impacted the Moon creating the iron-rich Luna Maria – the dark circular blotches on the face of the Moon, clearly visible to us even today. The Moon's magnetic rocks can also be traced back to Mars. They record a time when Mars was home to a working dynamo – a period when magnetized rocks were blasted off Mars and fell to the Moon. Large quantities of iron also fell to Earth – a process that continues to this day in the form of iron meteorites (and as shown micrometeorites). These are thought to originate from planetary cores of planetesimals. This is incorrect… *all* originate from the core of Mars. Moreover, a very recent accretion.

Photograph of the Hoba Meteorite, Grootfontein, Namibia. Hoba weighs about 66 tons and is 9 feet long by 9 feet wide by 3 feet thick. It is the largest single meteorite ever found and the largest piece of iron ever found near Earth's surface. It originated from the Martian core and fell to earth along with thousands of other iron meteorites (some of a stony-iron mix) only a few thousand years ago (700 BCE).

Source: Giraud Patrick, August 13, 2006.

For further reading on this may I recommend Alfred de Grazia's book, *The Iron Age of Mars*. Professor Grazia embraces Ackerman's Mercury form Mars theory and further proposes that the "terrible" Iron Age was a direct result of Earth's encounters with Mars which saw countless tons of iron, dust and debris fall from the sky; in some regions causing untold destruction and almost wiping out cultures. I would take this one step further and suggest virtually all iron formations on or near Earth's surface are the results of recent events in the heavens. This would include the world's vast reservoirs of Iron Ore – which incidentally are found in sedimentary rocks. They form layers that alternate with layers of silica and sometimes shale. No surprise given my ET stance.

Silica droplets from Mars = Chert (flint) deposits on Earth

The primary source of our sand was the vaporisation of tons of pure molten silica drawn up through the Valles Marineris and although large quantities of silica turned to vapour, great masses did not. It remained in a molten state and again fell back to the incandescent Mars (visualise an erupting volcano scaled up many thousand-fold). Today it forms part of the Martian bedrock as NASA's Curiosity rover is now finding out. Some silica globules were also flung out into space and found their way to Earth (along with chunks of molten iron, rock vapour, volatiles, dust and debris, etc.). It formed hard compact rocks we call chert or flint.

The definition of chert and flint can be confusing. Some say chert is light-coloured while flint is dark, but others say the opposite. Others call only the finest-quality materials flint and coarser stone chert. The most common definition limits flint to material formed in chalk deposits, while chert can come from limestone or other materials. The reader should not be concerned about the distinction. Chemically and structurally chert and flint are essentially the same. They are both made from almost pure silica, or silicon dioxide (SiO_2) – the exact same chemical composition as quartz sand.

Chert (flint) occurs in layers and irregular nodules in chalk and some other limestones. It is widely distributed around the world and was a primary material for Stone Age tools and weapons. Chert is usually either dull or semivitreous. It may have many colours, depending on the nature of impurities. Most common shades are grey, white, blue, green, yellow, black and red. Especially well-known occurrences of chert nodules are those found in chalks in Western Europe and North America. Chert is often bedded – rhythmically interlayered with chalk shale or in some cases hematite.

Left: Horizontal bands of nodular and sheet flints visible in the chalk cliff-face, Dover, UK. Right: The bulk of the beach pebbles (98 per cent) consists of flint and chert. Similar pebbles/stones can be found in garden soils. Glacial debris or ET?

Source: Author.

Left: Bootiful Paramoudras. These large and puzzling flint pot stones can be found at low tides on the beach below Beeston Bump (Beeston Regis Beach), Norfolk. Right: one of many flint circles on Beeston Regis Beach.

Source: Wikimedia commons.

Chert is everywhere yet *no one* knows how it formed! It is thought that it occurs as a result of chemical changes in compressed sedimentary rock formations, during the process of diagenesis. One hypothesis is that a gelatinous material fills cavities in the sediment, such as holes bored by crustaceans (sponges) or molluscs and that this becomes silicified. An idea that is at odds to the fact that in normal conditions silica is negligibly soluble in salt water. Peculiar conditions are required for silica to form from solution.

Actually, this whole line of thought is totally absurd for how do cavities left by burrowing sea creatures form chert layers? How did multiple layers form? Geology 101 deems layers are formed by deposits, a fact that seems to be ignored when it comes to the chert problem. Similarly, how can creatures be responsible for large flint circles or pot stones (with holes once filled with chalk) as seen in the images above? Where

235

are these illusive creatures? There must have been trillions of them. Were none of them fossilised? Fact: nowhere in the world is there evidence of flint (or chalk) being formed today, why is that?

As with the majority of material comprising Earth's crust, chert (nodules, pebbles, stones) is extraterrestrial – its source was the Martian mantle. Along with rock vapour, iron, dust and debris, great plumes of hot almost pure silica dioxide were flung out into space prior to, during and for many centuries after Mercury's birth. Large quantities were swallowed up by an insatiable Earth. A journey that probably involved some (not all) droplets solidifying into an amorphous glass-like structure (similar to obsidian rocks or tektites) – that is until encountering Earth's atmosphere where intense frictional heating caused the silica to re-melt, returning it to a soft jelly-like state. An alternative explanation may well be that close encounters saw the soft silica droplets sucked up from Mars more directly, along with water and volatiles. Either way, they fell in a soft jellylike state.

Molten silica dioxide fell from the sky in a variety of sizes ranging from pea-size, to giant boulders and gigantic clumps. Their shape was largely dictated by size; smaller pieces more rounded due to less air resistance – larger chunks, more elongated and nodular as a result of tumbling through the air. This is exactly what we see represented in chalks and many soils, especially in Europe – randomly shaped blobs of silica (chert) that have unquestionably fallen from above. They are essentially meteorites, but then again, so are most things covering Earth's surface.

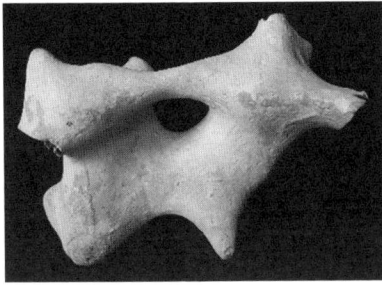

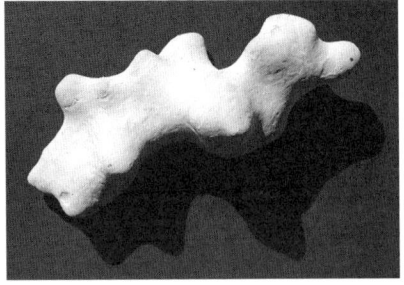

Randomly shaped extraterrestrial silicon dioxide droplets (approximately 6 or 7 inches in length) commonly known as chert/flint. The shape the result of tumbling through the atmosphere.

Source: Author.

There were times when wave after wave of fiery chert rained down on Earth – this is where we get the sedimentary beds from as in the image above – it is the only plausible explanation. Other times saw masses upon masses of molten silica quite literally poured down on earth. It remained molten and formed thick beds of chert and banded iron formations (BIFs, alternating layers of chert and iron oxides) similar to those found in the United States.

(Banded iron formations. https://en.wikipedia.org/wiki/Banded_ iron_formation*)*

The large pot stones or paramoudras (large flint concretions with a hollow centre) are explained thus; they are large spherical chunks of glutinous silica that were firstly flattened out into a pancake shape during their descent to Earth. The pancake widened and thinned, the onrush of air caused it to hollow out, like an upturned bag. The bag inflated beyond the ability of the silica's tension to hold it together and the central part shattered (producing yet smaller chert droplets), leaving behind the doughnut shape, which fell to Earth. The Paramoudras were probably quenched in shallow water. Although probably since moved and subjected to erosional processes, the deposits found on the Beeston Regis Beach (UK) are excellent specimens of extraterrestrial doughnuts.

The image below shows how raindrops undergo a very similar process as they fall through the air. I am proposing something very similar occurred with larger chunks of silica just prior to complete disintegration

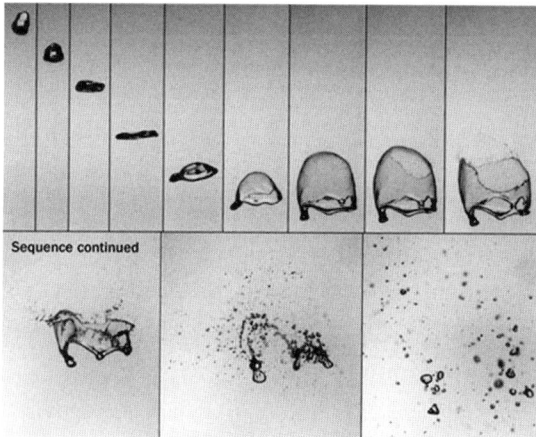

Falling water. Watch a water drop break apart in mid-air.
Source: Emmanuel Villermaux, http://www.dailymail.co.uk/ sciencetech/article-1201154/Solved-Why-raindrops-alike.html.

And then there's everything in between; some chunks falling to Earth in the process of forming a hole, while others fell intact and are responsible for the circular formations.

Comparisons can be made with tektites which come in a variety of shapes including oval "hamburger patty," sphere, dumbbell, a hollow-centred ball and teardrop (http:// astrobob.areavoices.com/2012/06/12/tektites-black-rocks-of-catastrophe/). I would imagine silica clumps formed very similar shapes. That said, we have to bear in mind that tektites are formed by rapid cooling as opposed to silica nodules, which were largely molten upon impact.

Chert is almost (99 per cent) pure silicon dioxide, the remainder impurities. The impurities are responsible for the variety of colours seen in chert. Black is down to organic compounds or metal sulfides, whereas various metal oxides and hydroxides bring about yellow, orange, brown, red, etc. These impurities were added as boiling hot molten silica mingled with other compounds on Mars (remember a drop of ink in a bucket of water is all it takes). Some chert has colour banding, indicative of a molten mix. In contrast, quartz grains gained their impurities as they crystallised out of the atmosphere.

Chert has a cryptocrystalline structure – quartz crystals so small they can only be seen with the aid of a high-power microscope. Slow cooling allows large crystals form, fast cooling yields smaller crystals. The fact that chert contains quartz crystals that are so tiny is consistent with rapid quenching. Just enough time during decent for submicroscopic crystals to form. I would imagine a matter of minutes and suggest experiments be carried out to see if I am correct. Bearing in mind past times saw an atmosphere at times supersaturated with water, dust and debris.

Often flint is found with a white crust or patina, which can be quite thick. This casing is white silica and has NO connection to the white chalk within which it is found.

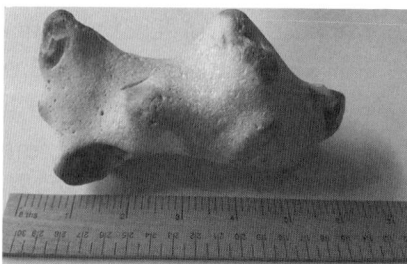

Left: Chert meteorite in chalk. Right: ET chert nodule with a thick whitish matt cortex (white silica, not chalk) extracted from chalk south coast UK. Looks very similar to the shape of a tumbling comet.

Source: Wikimedia Commons.

Chert is silicon dioxide, chalk is composed of calcium carbonate formed from the skeletons of trillions of micro-organisms. Question: if chert derives from burrowing sea creatures (siliceous sponges) by what process did the cortex form if having no association whatsoever with the chalk in which they lie? Also, not all chert has a cortex, how is this explained if the same processes were supposedly at work?

Although I'm not too sure about the process, chert nodules (pebbles, stones, etc.) gained their white patina as they tumbled to Earth. The fact that the cortex is said to be the same composition (silica) as the body is definitely telling us something. The most likely scenario is that we are looking at some kind of atmospheric quenching process. I would imagine that the surface of the molten droplets literally boiled as they fell – they were then subjected to various levels of quenching as they encountered the moisture laden troposphere (lowest layer). More water and/or a slower decent resulted in slower quenching and a thicker cortex – whereas less moisture produced less in the way of a cortex. Some chert may have been further quenched by terrestrial waters. It's possible that chert nodules devoid of a cortex originated from the ablation of larger silica chunks lower in the atmosphere, therefore less subjected to quenching by water. Or it may well be that they cooled sooner.

It is recommended that a few simple experiments be carried out to see if we are on the right track. We could start by slowly lowering a lump of boiling hot silica into a vat of water. If some kind of cortex forms then perhaps move on to actually replicating sizzling hot molten silica falling through a very damp environment. It is predicted that such experiments will prove very revealing.

Occasionally fossils can be found in chert and flint nodules, common examples are sea urchins, shells and sponges. Fossils can both be composed of original carbonate or re-crystallised quartz and may act as nuclei for nodule growth. Some flint pebbles may contain cavities assumed to be left by fossil sponges. Occasionally there may be silificified chalk fossils such as the echinoids Micraster, Echinocorys or some chalk bivalve or brachiopod. Certain types of chert also contain trapped fossilised marine flora.

As mentioned previously many life forms made it to Earth so there is no big surprise to find fossilised flora and fauna in chert.

Mars convulsed, its surface boiled and its oceans were subjected to continual evaporation and precipitation as they sloshed about the surface. Most plants and animals were incinerated (including humans). Some sea creatures (or the skeletal remains thereof) however, survived and made it to Earth. In this particular case, they got caught up in the steaming hot flood waters that repeatedly washed into the depths of the Valles Marineris where they mixed with molten silica – quantities of which were ejected and destined for Earth. It is predicted similar fossils to those found in chert (and other sedimentary rocks) will one day be discovered in the rock layers on Mars.

A brief word on chalk (limestone)

Chert is often found embedded in chalk, which naturally raises the question as to the origin of chalk. The current consensus deems it was laid down over many millions of years (80 million years plus) and yet, as with the formation of flint, nowhere in the world is there evidence of chalk being formed today… very perplexing. Could it too have fallen from the sky in the not-too-distant past? This is something I'm currently researching, however, my thoughts to date are as follows. Chalk is a soft white limestone made from the microscopic skeletons of marine plankton and the key to its origin lies with the boiling and evaporation of sea waters.

Boiling waters that turned to vapour – leaving behind a thick concentrated mushy blend of almost pure (99.9 per cent) calcium carbonate shells, or chalk. Now, did such events occur on Mars or Earth? The theme of this book leans towards the former. That is to say, chalk originated from Mars. Phases of the moist "heavenly mana" rained down in shallow waters to form layers of chalk intercalated with other sedimentary material, also largely from Mars.

The only connection flint has with chalk is that it was laid down during the same period. It has nothing whatsoever to do with the absurd notion of burrowing sea creatures or any other ad hoc explanation. Furthermore, the duration of the Cretaceous Period (chalk period) should be drastically condensed to just a few months and realigned to occurring just a few thousand years ago and not 65 million years ago as taught. But more on this in subsequent publications.

MYTHOLOGY

From a mythological perspective flint/chert finds a strong celestial association. For example, in Ancient Egypt flint is shown to be connected to the goddesses who are the (fiery) Eye of Re, with Re himself, the sky god Horus, snakes and lions. Flint is also related to the northern and eastern sky, storms and thunderbolts as well as luminosity! Additionally, both the sun and moon are linked with flint and shinning gold (http://discovery.ucl.ac.uk/1306709/1/1306709.pdf).

Note: At 1166 pages long this is the most comprehensive study of flint in Dynastic Egypt you will find.

> Flint is the symbol of thunder and lightning in nearly
> all American mythologies.
> (A Dictionary of Non-Classical Mythology,
> Edwardes, Mittal Publications, 1988)

One recent study suggests that there was an ideological orientation that associated all flint with the east, which itself was "associated with danger and difficulty, as well as solar creation, and is the birthplace of minerals" (http://www.birmingham.ac.uk/research/activity/connections/Essays/MMangum.aspx).

Now picture the following: a dark and stormy sky with hurricane-like winds – the sky roars like a ferocious lion as incessant thunder and lightning gives rise to luminous fiery stones (chert/flint) tumbling to Earth – most leaving a snake-like trail (silica vapour) in their wake.

It's not hard to see why silica meteors were associated with the sun in that as the stones burst forth from the heavens they lit up the sky like the sun, they were fiery and golden like the sun (Re). The lion trait may well be down to the deafening roar of the sky, it may equally be down to how the luminous bodies ferociously charged towards Earth, or a combination of both. The snake attribute is an easy one – it is similar to the snaking smoke trails left by some meteors today. They are due to high-altitude winds blowing the trail around – more often than not they are described as "snake-like". I cannot envisage such tumultuous events not creating thunder and lightning as the stones fells in a supersaturated atmosphere. If ancient cultures associate chert/flint with the northern or eastern sky, thunder and lightning, then we should take them at their word. As the evidence show, there were many phases of flint deposits, just as with our quartz sands.

Mythology or history?

Many of the last pages have essentially been directed towards promoting catastrophism from the geological aspect – the idea that the surface of the Earth has been shaped primarily not by incremental change but by sudden violent events – the extraterrestrial deposition of quartz sand being just one of these. I contend that the majority of the aforementioned events occurred during historical times, i.e. in the last 5,000 years. By way of demonstrating how and where they are written down I think it would be a good idea to dedicate the last few sections to ancient Egyptian mythology – although a better description would be ancient history.

The Red Sun – a solar system besieged with dust, debris and rock vapour

As the "Great light who shinest in the heavens" Re (Ra) was the Egyptian god of the Sun. He was typically represented as a sun-disc – such imagery points to the god's solar character. The solar disc features prominently in Egyptian art; it adorns almost every monument, tomb and temple wall throughout the Nile Valley. As the primary source of life such an ubiquitous representation is to be expected. However, there is something distinctly unusual about the way the Egyptians represented our nearest star that turns out to be incredibly revealing when placed in an environment of cosmic chaos. Re's most basic form consisted of a simple red disc. Why? Why not portray the Sun in all its blinding glory?

Left: Our blinding Sun. Right: An Egyptian Sun, a deep red disc (Note the encircling cobra which we will discuss shortly).

Source: Author.

The Sun is a blinding, golden-yellowish (if not near white) disc with emanating rays – a ball of golden glaring light. Surely everyone knows this – ask a child to paint the sun and they will invariably come up with a yellow circle with sun rays. A red disc is drab and lifeless by comparison, and yet Pharaonic Egypt reveals *not one* single golden Sun with a *complete* 360° sweep of sun rays. A perplexing situation, especially seeing how gold was believed to be the flesh of the gods and Re was the Sun god par excellence. What we should be seeing is a plethora of yellow Sun's drawn from the natural world. This is clearly not the case.

Cosmic chaos dictating every aspect of ancient life

Planetary upheaval results in a solar system enveloped in dust and debris, especially around the Sun – which became cocooned in a thick haze of orbiting dust. To picture this would be to place the Sun at the centre of a giant flat pancake of encircling dust and debris – very similar to the shape of a flying saucer as the dust somewhat settled out along the plane of the ecliptic. Shrouded in this melee we have the perpetrators of chaos, the errant planets. What this means is ancient cultures were in effect having to observe the sun through 93 million miles (distance between the Earth and the Sun) of "haze". What effect would this have on the appearance of the Sun?

In addition to the debris scattered about the solar system there's the dust in Earth's atmosphere to consider – close proximity planets and an expanding Earth gave rise to large-scale tectonic activity. In particular, the simultaneous eruption of numerous volcanoes, which led to the release of large amounts dust and gases into the air. Combine this with all the previously discussed cosmic debris (silica) falling to Earth over a 3,000-year period and we have an atmosphere laden with dust and gases (rock vapour, moisture, etc.). In short, to observe the sun in ancient times meant looking through a very thick wall of dust and gases.

It's pretty obvious what effect this had on the Sun – it appeared red, exactly as portrayed by the Egyptians. The Egyptians fashioned a red orb because the Sun appeared as a red orb, pure and simple. It is an iconic emblem that should be taken at face value (like so many others things Egyptian) as our ancient red sun rose in east, crossed the heavens as a red orb and set in the west as a red orb (chaos permitting). An obvious analogy would be a red Sun at sunset, caused by dust in the atmosphere – only ancient times saw the Sun hazed red throughout the day due to heaps more atmospheric and stellar dust.

Please note the distinctly unusual absence of anything resembling the simple phases of our *white* Moon in Egyptian art. Why? Because it is a recent edition – captured by Earth only a few thousand years ago.

The implications of a red Sun are both profound and very revealing. Many seemingly strange practices and beliefs can now be understood. An example would be the fact that ancient Egyptians were repeatedly depicted wearing nothing more than a loincloth. Something that can be confirmed by taking at almost any Egyptian relief, painting or otherwise; whether portraying workers in the field or soldiers following the pharaoh into battle, the figures are dressed in loincloths. A very puzzling situation. Egypt today has one of the hottest and sunniest climates in the world. During the summer months its average daily sunlight is twelve hours a day; it is incredibly hot and sunny. The intensity of the Sun is such that the Egyptian tourist board advises extreme caution. And yet, the ancients are shown wearing a simple loincloth. If the population of modern Egypt emulated the attire worn by the ancient Egyptians, they would be severely burnt – especially Bedouin tribes, who it could be said, lead a life more akin to the ancient Egyptians (outdoors).

In an attempt to explain this abnormality scholars have suggested that the artwork depicts an idealistic world (apparently, everything is idealised in ancient Egypt). In other words, the ancient Egyptians thought it would be a good idea to depict themselves engaging in battle or otherwise in the most impractical attire possible – something better suited to a beach in the Bahamas! The idea is absurd.

A veiled red Sun resulted in a totally different climate to that of today – it was a damp moist climate that allowed the Egyptians to wear nothing more than a loincloth without fear of getting sunburnt. It was a twilight world that allowed the ancient Egyptians to work tirelessly in the fields and build great monuments like the pyramids. Such activities could be carried out at any time during the day and throughout the year as there was no scorching orb to impede their work. Some would rightly say less energy from the Sun would lead to a cooler Earth. This wasn't the case in ancient times because a diminished red Sun was counter-balanced by tidal heating (tidal friction) brought about by the close proximity of Mars, Venus, Mercury and the subsequent capture of the Moon. I would also argue the electrical output from the Sun was far greater in ancient times due to a constant flow of debris falling into the Sun, which intensified the solar wind, which in turn, played a part in warming Earth.

A red Sun offers strong support for the presence of rock vapour in the atmosphere in that, to allow for the precipitation of quartz grains, the density of silica vapour must have been extremely high – and this must have had an effect on the Sun's appearance. Or, at the very least a contributing factor in hazing it red.

The dust and rock vapour enveloping Earth also affected the actual colour of the sky. In ancient Egypt the sky was a dominant sandy yellow (sometimes orangeish-red) as a direct result of the thick dense layer of rock vapour and iron impurities – the very source of our yellowish quartz grains. The clay and iron coating stage also playing a part in turning the sky yellow-red with understandably numerous variants, i.e. more iron would lead to a redder sky. Today on Mars, the presence of iron oxide in airborne dust particles is said to cause the sky to appear a bright orangeish-red colour during the day.

Such conditions led to the Egyptians rarely if ever experiencing a blue sky! It periodically appeared white, many times orangeish-red but predominantly yellow especially during intense periods of extraterrestrial sand deposition. Egyptian art reflects this since a good majority of scenes painted on temple, tomb and papyri show a dominance of background yellows and oranges. Examples would be scenes from the Egyptian Book of the Dead (see Falkner's BoD), or many of the tomb walls from the 19th Dynasty (Ramesside Period) where the background is exclusively yellow (Ancient Egyptian Art, Hartwig p264). Or may I recommend Gay Robin's book, *The Art of Ancient Egypt*, where again yellow skies dominate many of the images contained within. Incidentally, I associate the Ramesside Period to a time shortly after the birth of Mercury (Amarna Period) and the subsequent deposition of vast deposits of Saharan sand. Hence, the dominance of the colour yellow during this period.

Egyptologists would again reiterate the "idealistic" stance… That is to say, the Egyptians were able to fairly accurately represent a starry night (a dark blue/black sky with stars, of which there are many examples on tomb ceilings) but their imaginations took over when it came to daytime scenes. They somehow thought it would be preferable to have a red Sun traversing a yellow-orange sky than a natural golden Sun and blue skies. How weird?

There is nothing "idealised" about the sacred colours used in Egyptian art. Such a stance shows a poor understanding of our ancient forebears, whose legacy was one of trying to make sense of some very colourful but chaotic events. Background colours should be taken at face value as more often than not they are a historical representation of the actual colour of the sky, which was many times yellow.

It is interesting to note that there is no word for "blue" in ancient Greek. The Greeks called the sky Cronus, which is synonymous with bronze. In addition, Homer, writer of *The Iliad*, called it "shining like a bronze shield". Likewise, it wasn't just the Ancient Greeks who never said the sky was blue. None of the ancient languages had a proper word for blue! (http://www.theguardian.com/books/2010/jun/12/language-glass-colour-guy-deutscher)

Why bronze and not blue? Unless of course the sky actually maintained a bronze colour throughout Greek times – wouldn't surprise me in the least.

Some incredible observations but before that a quick word on the falcon sky god Horus. With a lack of insight and inability to comprehend cosmic chaos Egyptologists will tell you that Horus ("He who is above") was yet another imaginary aspect of the Sun, which is absurd. Horus was a totally separate entity to Re and Egyptian text support this (i.e. Re talking to Horus – how can a god talk to itself?). Horus and his many forms should be identified with the reigning planetary bodies as they loomed larger than the Sun. That being said, it's a little more complicated than that as it involves a further association with Egypt's divine royal family who believed they were "at one" with celestial bodies. It is beyond the scope of this book to explain further in any great detail. In the interest of progressing, we will keep it simple and where applicable refer to the planets in chaos as Horus bodies or similar. For more information, I refer the reader to my previous works, The God King Scenario (GKS). Now, back to our red sun.

Just as we can look a reddened Sun at sunset or sunrise today, ancient cultures were able to look directly at the Sun throughout the day as there was no blinding glare – a unique set of circumstances that led to some awe-inspiring observations. For instance, prior to settling into their present locations, the Horus bodies Mars, Venus, Mercury and the Moon (and many other smaller bodies now since swallowed up by the Sun and/or the planets) frequently appeared to take up a position between the Earth and the Sun. In other words, they appeared during the day – they were clearly seen courtesy of a red Sun, even at midday. This would be especially so of the "winged messenger" Mercury and Comet Venus which were seen for eons as they slowly settled between the Sun and the Earth (daytime). A cloaked Sun also meant that some planets such as Jupiter (Ptah) were occasionally seen on the other side of the sun, i.e. at superior conjunction. A sight to behold.

Not only were the planets visible during the day as incandescent red orbs, they also took on the appearance of Re. Indeed, under the authority and guardianship of the sky god Horus (*not* the sun), the planets joined a celestial realm of red orbs. They were accordingly adorned with a string of divine epithets such as "offspring of Re", "Appearing like Re", "Likeness of Re", "Chosen by Re", "Shining like Re" and "Rising like Re", plus many more. Such titles should be taken at face value as they are clearly alluding to celestial bodies taking on the attributes of the Sun, a red Sun. It is the very reason why the red disc features so prominently in Egyptian art. Given the celestial arrangement I would even go so far as to say the majority of Sun's represented in Egyptian art were not the Sun! (More on this shortly).

Wadjet, the Fire-Spitting Uraeus – Protector of Re (Sun) and the Horus planets

Another consequence of a red Sun was naked-eye observations of solar phenomena we've only recently discovered (in the 1970s). I am referring to coronal mass ejections (CMEs), flares and prominences. Coronal mass ejections are explosions in the Sun's corona that spew out solar particles. A lot of material is thrown out into the solar wind. Coronal mass ejections can be dangerous when they hit the Earth, endangering astronauts, disrupting long-distance radio communications and causing strong geomagnetic storms, aurorae (northern and southern polar lights) and electrical power blackouts. CMEs usually happen independently, but are sometimes associated with solar flares.

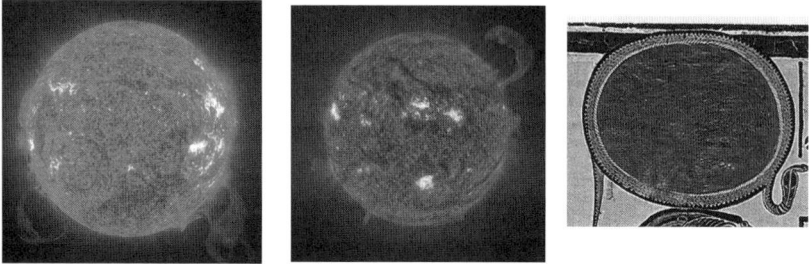

Left: Photos of the Sun taken by NASA's SOHO spacecraft. Right: Typical Egyptian "sun" with encircling cobra. What does this represent?

If I may draw the reader's attention to the image of the Sun on the left taken by NASA's SOHO spacecraft. The Sun's glare has been filtered out so what we are looking at is an incandescent red orb with a gigantic CME striking out from the top right-hand corner of the Sun's surface. Other smaller prominences can be seen emanating from the corona; the lower left would be one such example. The bright *golden* flashes are flares. Prominences are often described as "snakelike". For example, on May 1, 2015, Phys.org published an article with the title "Video: An enormous plasma snake erupts from the Sun". They followed with:

Over the course of April 28–29 a gigantic filament, briefly suspended above the surface of the sun, broke off and created an enormous snakelike eruption of plasma that extended millions of miles out into space. [Note: filaments ejected out into space are also called CMEs]

http://phys.org/news/2015-05-video-enormous-plasma-snake-erupts.html#jCp

Similar NASA videos can be found online.

Describing CMEs and prominences as snakelike is natural since they literally take on the attributes of a rearing snake striking out (how else would you describe them?). Turning to the image on the right we have a typical Egyptian Sun – like so many other suns it is adorned with a snake which encircles the main body. Now, if we compare the two images the symbolism becomes stark-staringly obvious – it is apparent that the Egyptians observed similar snakelike prominences lashing out from the sun and this was embodied in the cobra. There was no need for special light filters or occulting discs as thick dust and rock vapour had the same effect of filtering out the Sun's glare. It enabled the Egyptians to directly observe solar phenomena thousands of years before us. In support of this let us take a look at the deified form of the cobra, the goddess Wadjet.

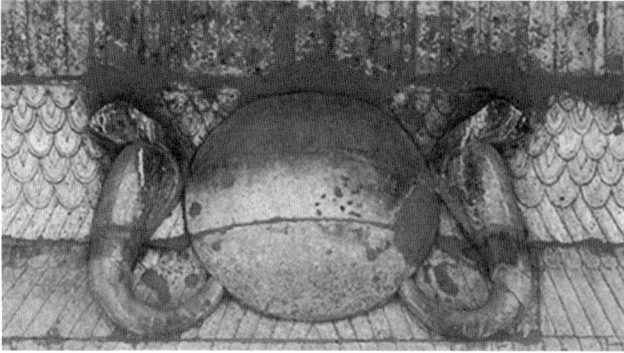

Wadjet, the Fire Spitting Uraeus (cobra)

Taking pride and place on the forehead of the divine royal family as well as draped over numerous solar discs, Wadjet in the form of the cobra, has to be among some of the most familiar and iconic emblems for ancient Egypt, it is literally everywhere. Its solar association is well known.

"Re arises, his uraeus upon him...."

(Utterance 298, R. O. Faulkner, The ancient Egyptian Pyramid Texts)

Even before its identification with the king, the cobras protective attributes were recognised, and it was identified as the eye of Re, sometimes protecting his solar disc by spitting fire and venom. (Dictionary of Ancient Egypt p67 Shaw & Nicholson)

Snakes do not spit fire! The only fire-spitting serpents were the ones observed striking out from the Sun (and the planets). Such actions were naturally perceived as a protective attributes. Egyptian text confirms the fire-spitting protective traits:

> My vision is cleared, my heart is in its proper place, my uraeus (cobra) is with me every day. I am Re, who himself protects himself, and nothing can harm me.
> (Book of the Dead, Faulkner p.58)

> This is the fire which shines behind Re and which is concentrated behind him.
> (Spell 136b BoD 126)

Wadjet's epithets further confirm my solar phenomena identification. Examples would include: "She of the Fiery Eye", as great golden bursts of energy struck out from the Sun (revealing the true meaning of "the flesh of the gods"). "The Lady of Devouring Flame" is self-explanatory. "Goddess of the Placenta" as the Sun's "inners" raged with activity. "She who Loves Silence" is interesting inasmuch as we can imagine unremitting prominences striking out from Re but, when viewed from Earth… just a silent spectacle. Much like watching solar activity on a NASA video.

Re (Ra) wasn't the only body to invoke the protective services of the goddess Wadjet. On the contrary, the surface of most "Horus" bodies (the planets) exhibited similar striking out traits as their father Re. This, however, was more to do with volcanism than violent ejections of plasma. Mars, once again playing a pivotal role.

Mars, Mars and mainly Mars again

Returning to the Egyptian "sun" above, the colours shown are as follows. The main body is a vibrant red. Surrounding this is a thin white band followed by the serpent's main body which is yellow and contains reddish specs. A serrated black outline completes the image (see my web or a web search). Similar "suns" (less detailed) abound the length and breadth of the Nile Valley but do they all represent the Sun? If so, what exactly do the colours mean? Why the yellow ring? If our Sun was seen to strike out why not a red cobra emanating from a red disc?

As discussed, not all red orbs were the Sun. Far from it, and this is most certainly the case with the ubiquitous yellow ringed orbs. Even allowing for a little symbolism they are in fact very close to, if not an actual portrayal of Mars as seen in ancient skies (to a lesser extent Venus, Mercury and the Moon). Let me explain.

The surface of Mars, a writhing, seething cauldron of molten rock and metal; it glowed red from the effects, hence the red disc. The surface temperature at times became white-hot causing the white ring above the surface. The high temperatures gave rise to an atmosphere dense with vaporised rock (the source of our sand), which appeared yellow (silica vapour with iron impurities), prompting the yellow circle, or corona. The rocky yellow corona seemed to come alive as Mars convulsed and ejected plumes of material and vapour out into space. These silent prominences looked very much like the venomous snakes observed striking out from the Sun. Such actions were naturally perceived as the "Fiery Eyed Cobra" protecting the god Horus/Mars. Indeed another common epithet of the "Daughter of Re" Wadjet was the "Protector of Horus". A very appropriate descriptive title.

The red specs in the sandy-coloured atmosphere derive essentially from debris not only blasted into the air but also falling back to Mars – burning up and punching holes in the swirling atmosphere in the process. From Earth, another silent spectacle, in actuality hell on Mars. Once again, is it any wonder all signs of life have been obliterated?

The origin of the serrated black outline is a little less clear. However, I will offer a few suggestions. It may well represent darker patches seen blotting the upper atmosphere of Mars brought about by cooler temperatures. Similar to sunspots, although at temperatures of roughly 3,000 to 4,500 K (2,700 to 4,200 °C) contrast with the surrounding material at about 5,780 K (5,500 °C) which leaves sunspots clearly visible as black spots. Alternatively, it may well represent the blackness of space, so it could be a night scene. Similar serrations can be found on the body of Re's perennial adversary, the serpent/snake god Apep (Apophis = Jetstream) who was a god of darkness and chaos, there may be connection. Perhaps the solar wind played a part and as it enveloped Mars the outer rim actually looked black. It could also be a simple case of artistic license and what we're looking at is just a black outline. There are many possibilities.

In a nutshell, the goddess Wadjet derived initially from observations of solar prominences striking out from our red

Sun. It followed that red Horus bodies exhibited very similar traits (largely due to volcanism) so they too were perceived to be protected by the "Great Serpent".

Incandescent oblate "Horus" spheroids rule the heavens

Supporting evidence for the notion that we are looking at Mars and not the Sun comes to us via the shape of the Horus disc(s) – which is an oblate spheroid (a sphere that is squashed at its poles and swollen at the equator). The question is why?

When seen through surface fog, light hazy cloud or even hazed on the horizon, the Sun is a perfect circular orb. So why didn't the Egyptians draw a perfect disc? Drawing a circle is very easy – even a large one merely requires a piece of string, a peg and a marker (if that). An oblate spheroid on the other hand is slightly more difficult – more effort is required to squash a sphere and make it look right. So why did the Egyptians go to the trouble of doing this?

Religion guided every aspect of Egyptian life, the sun god Ra was held in the highest esteem. Why fashion an imperfect, squashed red sphere with a "spitting" yellow ring round it if not an actual attribute of the sun? Wouldn't it make much more sense to represent the sun god par excellence with a perfect circle, an immaculate divine disc? A glaring orb with sunrays as seen today?

A perplexing situation especially when considering how the Sun not only appears as a perfect sphere it is physically a perfect sphere!

After fifty years of research, we've discovered a strange, beautiful fact about our Sun: it's more perfectly round than anything else in the natural world. It's not the roundest in a certain category; it's just the roundest sphere there is. If it were a beach ball, *The Guardian* writes, it would be a hair's width away from complete perfection (http://www.popsci. com/science/article/2012-08/sun-more-perfect-naturally-occurring-sphere-universe). [Note: prior to this discovery in Aug 2012 astronomers firmly believed the sun was an oblate spheroid.]

What this means is, even if the Sun was hazed behind a wall of dust as I contend, it would still "mainly" (more on this shortly) appear as a perfect sphere. Even more so because no glare deems Re was seen throughout the day, chaos permitting of course.

The sun's true spherical shape captured at sunset.
Source: Wikimedia Commons.

The planets on the other hand are oblate! The shape of Mars today is an oblate spheroid; its equatorial diameter is higher than its polar diameter (pole to pole). The other planets (including Earth and the Moon) in our solar system are also oblate spheroids with Saturn being the most oblate. The planets today are mere specks in the night sky but what if another bout of chaos brought mars close to earth to loom larger than the Moon? What shape would it be?

It is becoming glaringly obvious that the squashed red orb with its enveloping yellow atmosphere derived from direct observations of an incandescent oblate Mars (and other bodes) as it dominated ancient skies. It is the only logical conclusion. It does not symbolise the sun – because even if hazed, the sun doesn't have a yellow ring around it. Moreover, the Egyptians would never depict the sun god in such an imperfect way, especially when considering how it graces our skies today as a perfect sphere. As in so many cases the ancients portrayed what they saw. I would even argue that the seething silica-based atmosphere is accurately represented and proportioned.

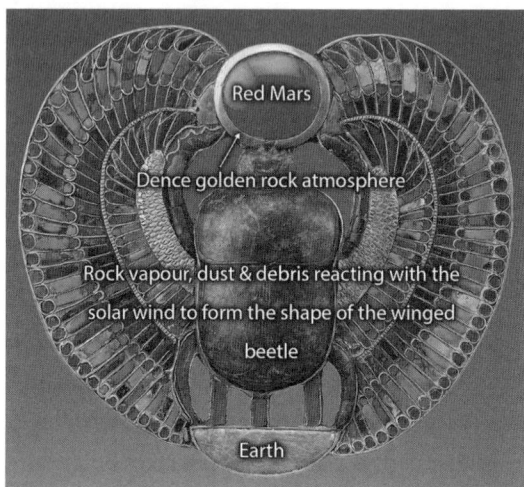

Tutankhamun's Pectoral. Just one of many frequent manifestations of Mars. In this particular case we have a red hot oval shaped Mars enclosed in a seething golden rocky atmosphere. The winged beetle (Khepre, "He who has come into being") formed as the solar wind stripped volatiles, dust, debris and rock vapour from Mars as it interacted with Earth's atmosphere. The Egyptians didn't imagine the above, they saw it!

Source: Wikimedia Commons.

It is an irrefutable fact that the red disc dominates Egyptian art – and the majority are oblate spheroids. They come in a variety of sizes and adornments. Some have outstretched wings attached (winged disc), others are surmounted by cow's horns (goddesses Isis or Hathor) or plumed feathers (see Comet Venus), some have both. Most discs have a cobra draped over them (the head and tail of the snake protruding from the disc) or the cobra fully encircles the disc, as we have seen. A diligent search will elicit some near perfect circular discs and some can be found coloured yellow or orange, however, these are few and far between (certainly none with a *complete* set of sunrays). Overall, the red oblate spheroid reigns supreme, literally. The reader may confirm this for themselves by taking a look at almost any aspect of Egyptian art. [Note; the distinct lack of a white crescent or full Moon.]

These very same flattened discs are inextricably linked to the "Lord of the Sky", the god Horus and his many forms. Indeed, if you are looking at the red disc you are invariably looking at the disc of Horus and less so the disc of Re. The imagery and sacred text clearly reflect this (but unfortunately for us, Egyptologists naively believe Horus was just one of many numerous aspects of the Sun). With this in mind, the assumption has to be that the majority of discs/spheres/orbs (carved, painted or otherwise) represent the planets in chaos, in particular Mars. Mars set many precedents in regards to the whole mytho-theology of ancient Egypt – it is the very reason why the oblate red disc was so prevalent throughout Egypt.

But where does that leave our red Sun? While it was undoubtedly seen and imaged the question is, to what extent? In the absence of any textual reference, perhaps some of the more circular discs represent the Sun, however, they may also signify errant planets as they too may have occasionally looked circular due to a molten state.

Actually, despite what was said earlier the Sun can occasionally look slightly oval when near the horizon. More so during summer sunset. It is caused by the refraction of light through the atmosphere. As the Sun sets, the light emitted must pass through an increasingly thick layer of air, which tends to bend the light rays away from the horizon. The bottom of the Sun is closer to the horizon than the top, so the effect becomes more pronounced, making the Sun appear squished and oblate. In actuality, the sun has already set and the light rays are being refracted from below the horizon into the position we see while observing this effect.

Perhaps some of the oblate discs are the setting Sun? While I'm prepared to accept to the possibility of a small percentage as being the Sun, it would be just that, a mere fraction – for the following reasons. If in anyway the setting Sun, then the distinct lack of "normal" golden glaring suns has to be explained. They should totally outnumber anything resembling an oval setting sun, yet there are none! The circular golden disc should be the dominant symbol especially when remembering how gold was the "Flesh of the Gods" and representative of the sun god. In addition, if the setting Sun, why the encircling yellow band?

I think perhaps a little recapping is in order: the majority of solar discs (oblate or otherwise) belong to the deity

Horus and by extension, the planets in chaos (Mars, Venus, Mercury and the Moon = Horus bodies). Close proximity planets are directly responsible for the oblate discs found in almost every aspect of Egyptian art (including the scared hieroglyphs). Some oblate discs may be the Sun. This, however, has more to do with the domination of the oblate planets and borrowed symbolism than the Sun actually appearing squashed. Thick silica vapour, dust and debris in Earth's atmosphere further contributed to the squashed look as Horus bodies traced out a similar path to the Sun – many times setting in the dust-laden west. The prominence of Horus with more earthly affairs is consistent with oblate discs dominating the heavens and looming larger than the Sun/Re.

Mars, the main perpetrator of planetary upheaval took on various forms as it was systematically torn apart. Many of these manifest in the different forms of Horus (wings, horns, plumes, etc.). Central to the physical appearance of Mars was the oblate red disc with a yellow circle, the primary source of our sand. Tidal friction, the eruption of thousands of volcanoes, combined with ceaseless internal convulsions and Mercury's birth turned the surface of Mars into a seething ocean of glowing liquid rock. Tons of which vaporised and swathed the planet in a thick, hot, dense silica-based atmosphere, manifest in the yellow ring.

As Mars convulsed it spat forth from the fiery ring enormous snakelike plumes of virtually pure silica droplets and vapour – the source of Earth's flint and quartz sand deposits (and a pinch of feldspars). In particular, the more recent unconsolidated sandy deposits of the Sahara and Arabian deserts. The snakelike apparitions were naturally viewed as the cobra encircling and protecting the disc of Horus/Mars – the Egyptian's duly pinned a snake's head and tail to the dynamic encircling yellow rim where appropriate.

The purpose of the last few pages was to demonstrate how planetary chaos dominated the ancient world and how it is in plain sight for all to see – a necessary inclusion if I'm to prove that Mars was the primary source of our sand. We have seen how something as innocuous as a solar disc turns out to be incredibly revealing upon closer inspection. A tenet of my thesis that, if correct, has severe implications for Earth's more recent history. But we've only just scratched the surface and as the reader will appreciate there is so much more to this – far too much to include here. For more information on the "how and where" I refer the reader to my previous works. There you will find a plethora of material including that of where it is written down that Mercury was birthed from Mars (Amarna Period), in addition to the physical identification of Egypt's more prominent gods. As I said at the start of the book, the ancient Egyptians have, in effect, laid the whole thing out for us.

BIBLIOGRAPHY

Ackerman, J. (1999), *Firmament: Recent Catastrophic History of the Earth*, Infinity Publishing.

Ackerman, J. (1999)*, Chaos: A New Solar System Paradigm*, Infinity Publishing.

Alfred de Grazia. (2009), *The Iron Age of Mars*, Metron Publications.

Brink. (1985), *Engineering Geology of Southern Africa, Volume 4*, Pretoria.

Chronic, H. (1983), *Roadside Geology of Arizona*, Mountain Press Publishing Company.

Crawford, J. (1988), *Zion National Park - Towers of Stone*, Zion National History Association.

Cooke, Warren, Goudie. (1993), *Desert Geomorphology*, CRC Press; First Edition.

Dickinson, W. W. & Ward, J. D. (1994), *Low depositional porosity in eolian sands and sandstones, Namib desert*, Journal of Sedimentary Research.

Edwardes, M. (1988), *A Dictionary of Non-Classical Mythology*, Mittal Publications.

Elias & Mock. (2013), *Encyclopedia of Quaternary Science, 2nd Edition,* Elsevier.

Faulkner, R. (1989), *The Ancient Egyptian Book of the Dead*, British Museum Press, London.

Faulkner, R. (1994), *Egyptian Book of the Dead: Book of Going Forth by Day,* Chronicle Books, California.

Maurette, M. (2006), *Micrometeorites and the Mysteries of Our Origins,* Springer.

Pettijohn, F. J.; Potter, Paul E.; Siever, Raymond. (1987), *Sand and Sandstone,* Springer Science.

Pye & Tsoar. (2009), *Aeolian Sand and Sand Dunes*, Springer.

Shaw, I., Nicholson, P. (2002), *The British Museum Dictionary of Ancient Egypt*, British Museum Press, London.

Shurki, N. M. (1945), *Geology of the Nubian Sandstone,* Nature Publishing Group.

Warren, A. (2013), *Dunes: Dynamics, Morphology,* History, Wiley-Blackwell.

Websites, if not contained in the book.

Documentary. How the earth was made.
http://www.history.com/shows/how-the-earth-was-made/
videos/how-the-earth-was-made-sahara

Professor Charlie Bristow
http://www.bbk.ac.uk/geology/our-staff/charlie-bristow

Dr. Farouk El-Baz
http://www.bu.edu/remotesensing/faculty/el-baz/

Evolution of Sand Seas
http://www.bu.edu/remotesensing/files/pdf/398.pdf

A Reality Check on Flood Geology. Timothy K. Helble.
http://www.csun.edu/~vcgeo005/Helble.pdf

Nubian Sandstone (Hermina 1990; Klitzsch and Wycisk
1999)
http://sundoc.bibliothek.uni-halle.de/diss-
online/07/07H178/t4.pdf

Sand Atlas
http://www.sandatlas.org/

Review of the potential host rocks for radioactive waste
disposal in the southern Piedmont.
http://sti.srs.gov/fulltext/DP-MS-81-96.pdf

Origin of Lower Cretaceous ('Nubian') sandstones of North-east Africa and Arabia from detrital zircon U-Pb SHRIMP dating
http://earth.huji.ac.il/Data/File/dov/Kolodneretal2009.pdf

Ackerman J
http://www.firmament-chaos.com/

Dr Mathew Genge, Imperial College London.
http://www.imperial.ac.uk/people/m.genge

INDEX